Cyberstrategy

The Chartered Institute of Marketing/Butterworth-Heinemann Marketing Series is the most comprehensive, widely used and important collection of books in marketing and sales currently available worldwide.

As the CIM's official publisher, Butterworth-Heinemann develops, produces and publishes the complete series in association with the CIM. We aim to provide definitive marketing books for students and practitioners that promote excellence in marketing education and practice.

The series titles are written by CIM senior examiners and leading marketing educators for professionals, students and those studying the CIM's Certificate, Advanced Certificate and Postgraduate Diploma courses. Now firmly established, these titles provide practical study support to CIM and other marketing students and to practitioners at all levels.

The Chartered Institute of Marketing

Formed in 1911, The Chartered Institute of Marketing is now the largest professional marketing management body in the world with over 60,000 members located worldwide. Its primary objectives are focused on the development of awareness and understanding of marketing throughout UK industry and commerce and in the raising of standards of professionalism in the education, training and practice of this key business discipline.

Books in the series

Forthcoming

Cyberstrategy

Business strategy for extranets, intranets and the internet

Pauline Bickerton, Matthew Bickerton and Kate Simpson-Holley

Published in association with
The Chartered Institute of Marketing

OXFORD AUCKLAND BOSTON JOHANNESBURG MELBOURNE NEW DELHI

Butterworth-Heinemann
Linacre House, Jordan Hill, Oxford OX2 8DP
225 Wildwood Avenue, Woburn, MA 01801-2041
A division of Reed Educational and Professional Publishing Ltd

R   A member of the Reed Elsevier plc group

First published 1998
Reprinted 1999

British Library Cataloguing in Publication Data
A catalogue record for this book is available from the British Library

ISBN 0 7506 4203 3

Typeset by Avocet Typeset, Brill, Aylesbury, Bucks
Printed and bound in Great Britain by Biddles Ltd,
Guildford and King's Lynn

Contents

Acknowledgements

We would like to extend a warm thank you to all our clients who gave their permission for their experiences to be included in Cyberstrategy.

We would also like to thank Rachael Bickerton for her superb legal contribution to the book (please see the Appendix).

Lastly we would also like to thank the whole of MarketingNet for their patience and support as this really was a team effort even though only three of us are mentioned as the authors!

Chapter 1

Introduction

Where should your organization invest? Internet, Extranet or Intranet?

This book seeks to offer a strategic approach to the issues facing all organizations wanting to adopt Internet technology in order to generate measurable business solutions. Corporations have traditionally been left to determine how to approach this new technology without access to any strategic expertise.

In the past companies would tend to approach an Internet supplier, a marketing company or a consultancy firm. The Internet company would typically focus on the technological requirements and fail to see the business or marketing implications. A marketing company would often focus on the design and promotion but not provide innovative technical or strategic recommendations. Consultants might offer strong strategic recommendations but without the practical steps needed to fulfil these objectives. They often take a global view and investigate the business case for the investment, providing great insight into the marketplace and commercial strategy but neglecting the technological, marketing or practical needs of the project.

MarketingNet is one of the leading Internet Marketing organizations in the UK today. Working at a strategic level with a large number of blue chip organizations, all three authors are practitioners of both Internet consultancy and implementation. Directly out of this work combining the theoretical and practical elements of Internet development and marketing, we have evolved a strategic framework to enable organizations to conceptualize the match between the benefits of the technology and the needs of their business. The power of this methodology is that it is functionally independent and can be used across an organization to plan, implement and manage the technology effectively.

One of the major issues for any manager today is accessing the right strategic information at the same time as the practical details needed to generate a successful Internet project plan. Without the basic knowledge of how the Internet will work in practice, one cannot identify the full power and potential for the theoretical strategy that must be determined before a project gets underway. For example, if the keywords that will promote your site online are wrong for your target market, it could undermine your whole strategic proposition. Strategic decisions are too often taken at a high level and then not communicated to the implementers of the plan, creating a situation in which the overall mission is lost amongst all the practical considerations. *Cyberstrategy* will help you to avoid the pitfalls.

Figure 1.1 illustrates the dilemma facing decision-makers looking at Internet technology for the first time. There are a variety of areas that must be considered if a thorough investigation of the potential of the technology is to be achieved.

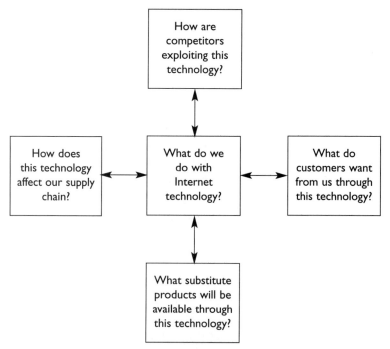

Figure 1.1   What decisions does your organization face?

It is crucial to know what your competitors are already doing, how you can match and better them and provide something of value to your clients. Of course this must relate to and support the long-term aims of your business.

Cyberstrategy seeks to break the stalemate decision-making process that lies between what can be done and what might be done. The Cyberstrategy Model, described in the next chapter, is a tool developed directly as a result of working closely with a wide range of innovative companies. You will be able to apply your own business and situation to the model, locating where you are and where you might take your organization in the future.

By diagnosing what you would like to achieve and why, you can look at problems from a variety of different perspectives to ensure that you are well equipped to develop a coherent and successful planned approach to this new technology, or to evaluate work that you have already done. The model is flexible and will apply equally to different industry types to create a generic structure that will guide you through each stage of Internet implementation.

Cyberstrategy does not intend to be prescriptive, but to provide you with the essential knowledge and tools you will need to fully assess and evaluate your Internet potential in line with the rest of your industry. The aim is to give you access to the essential targets that will focus attention on the crucial areas where decisions can have the greatest impact on the long-term success of the project.

The book is accompanied by a number of online resources designed to help develop these ideas. Supportive case studies are available at www.marketingnet.com/cyberstrategy to help illustrate how various companies have exploited different areas of Internet technology to develop their own business aims and achieve not only long-term solutions but real, quantifiable benefits including profit generation and rationalization of internal structures and procedures. In addition, there is an online discussion forum in which questions and contributions can be posted that is exclusively managed by the authors. This is only for readers of the book, so do have it close to hand as you will be asked questions with reference to specific text in *Cyberstrategy* as your password to enter this extranet.

The authors are all available via email on strategy@marketingnet.com if you have any specific queries or comments that you would like to make. Here, we would welcome any comments that you may have and will happily respond to your queries or suggestions.

Chapter 2

The cyberstrategy model

Bridging the gap between marketing and IT through strategic planning

Every organization in the world today is wrestling with the question 'How can Internet technology improve my business?' Each organization, whether large or small, is confronted with the issue of how to integrate the Internet into the way they do business – but at what cost and to what benefit?

At one extreme, some organizations decide to allocate a small budget to secure their stake in the ground. They see the venture just as a necessary cost and expect little return on their investment. They wait for the technology to mature and for the business case to be more clearly evident.

At the other extreme, some organizations implement radical and high-risk projects that are pioneering for their industry sector. They wrestle with how best to manage the initiative and how best to exploit the benefits of this new technology. Their groundbreaking efforts can, however, often be expensive and detract from core business.

The next issue is, 'who is responsible?' In many blue chip organizations, a battle has ensued between Marketing and IT as each vies for ownership and control. This chapter helps you decide where your organization is best suited to start.

There are no right or wrong answers; there is no panacea. Only the organization concerned can decide how appropriate Internet technology is to improving their business and who is best suited to implement it. However, is there any framework

Stages \ Uses	Internet	Extranet	Intranet
Presentation			
Interaction			
Representation			

Figure 2.1   The Cyberstrategy Model

to making conceptualizing it easier? Are there any tools or methodologies to help?

We now introduce the Cyberstrategy Model and explain how this could help.

The model is a three by three grid. The columns represent the use of Internet technology and the rows represent the stage of development of the technology.

On the top, we describe the use to which Internet technology is being put:

1 Internet – the general public. This is a broad term, which describes the general public communications network. In the context of this book, we are using it to mean an Internet site published publicly under an organization's own name: www.thecompany.co.uk or www.company.com

2 Extranet – a select audience. This term relates to the use of net-worked or Internet technology (browser based) specifically for an intended invited audience which is often suppliers, customers and/or agents. It is secured so that the general public does not have access. In some cases this implies a private network and in other cases an Internet site with security (e.g. password protection).

3 Intranet – within the organization. This term relates to the use of networked or Internet technology (browser based) specifically for communicating to personnel within the organization. Again, it can be a private network (e.g. a wide area network using Microsoft Exchange or Lotus Domino) or an internal secured web server where the Internet is used only as a cost-effective connection system.

Down the side we describe the various stages of implementation:

1 Presentation. This is where you publish information. This then does one of the following:

   - provides an image
   - imparts knowledge and values
   - gives access to information
   - illustrates products or services.

   It may provide a call to action but is most easily understood as an electronic brochure, newsletter, magazine, advertising hoarding or TV commercial.

2 Interaction. This means there is a two-way communication. The system asks questions and the user then supplies answers. The answers then lead on to more specific information. This is where the use of Internet technology steps out of the bounds of being an electronic publishing tool.

3 Representation. This is where the organization replaces elements of its activities. The technology performs a business process otherwise undertaken by a person or persons. This could be any activity across the organization from sourcing inputs into producing a sales channel.

The next section of this chapter introduces the use of this matrix for strategic decision making. We are providing an overview of the business benefits each of the boxes in Figure 2.1 could potentially provide to an organization. We then go on to take a closer examination of the three applications – Internet, Extranet and Intranet – by dedicating a chapter to each. At this point, each chapter goes into the subtle differences and resulting issues each brings.

The matrix is used in this chapter to provide an overview. By taking each of the uses of the technology and matching it to the stage of the development we provide a chef's tour of the business benefits.

The power of this model is that it structures and segments all the issues which are normally grouped together. By developing a model like this for your organization, you will have a clear understanding of where the best return on investment is likely to come.

Key to the model is the concept of jumping across applications of the technology. Organizations who start with Internet may wish to consider Extranets next before developing Internet applications further. Likewise, organizations may choose to develop Intranets first and then publish out into Extranets and then to the Internet. The model lays a matrix for strategic mapping of business benefits over timeframes and investment levels. More about what are the best routes across the matrix are given within each of the chapters dedicated to Internets, Extranets and Intranets.

To provide a complete overview, we have mapped below some overall benefits of the application of each Internet technology against the level to which it has been deployed. We outline the business benefits of each stage of development against the application of the technology (Figure 2.2 is to give you a sense of overview). We then move down each application to look at the benefits of each stage of development.

Stages \ Use	Internet	Extranet	Intranet
Presentation	International presentation and positioning: name and image, products and services	Cost-effective fast publication of material to a specific target audience	Consistent corporate communication managed centrally
Interaction	Two-way communication with the visitor	Channel which elicits feedback and communication with specific target audience	Open communication channel across the organization
Representation	Cost-effective sales and order processing	Cost-effective targeted selling Replacement to a core business activity	The benefits of remote working

Figure 2.2   An overview of the business benefits of the varying applications and stages of development of networked or Internet technology

What is the business case for Internets?

The business case for stage 1 – Internet presentation

1 The Internet is gradually becoming a necessary business cost. It could be said that producing an Internet presence (presentation) is no longer an option for most organizations: when the rest of your industry is experimenting with new media, it makes sense for your company to get involved as well. But why?

2 It is an international directory listing that enables both existing and potential customers to have easy access to information about your company. The Internet has become the phone book to the world. The benefits of enlisting increase in proportion to the global coverage of your organization. For international organizations, the Internet provides the first opportunity to produce a truly global brochure that can be quickly and easily kept up to date.

3 An opportunity to differentiate yourself publicly and explicitly from your competitors. The Internet allows users to compare suppliers side by side. This gives you the unique opportunity, and the challenge, to stand out from the crowd and compete head-on with other companies. With the speed of the Internet, we estimate that you have just four seconds to communicate why you are different and entice someone into your site. For some organizations, the main benefit of this technology is that it sharpens their focus on their market positioning.

The business case for stage 2 – Internet interaction

1 You are creating a cost-effective sales person. Your Internet site can enable a potential client to navigate through a decision tree and allow your organization to lead them to the exact information, product or service they require. An interactive site can then encourage the user to take action and make a direct enquiry. The advantage for the client is that they can explore all potential products and services at their leisure without feeling any pressure from a sales person. For your organization, this is powerful because the enquiry will contain the exact route the client took through the sales process – generating a record of the enquiry which provides further evidence of the client's needs and interests.

2 You are creating a cost-effective communication channel to gain feed-

back from customers. This can have implications for anything from market research to the test marketing of future products or services. You have the means to create user panels, talk to your customers easily and gather valuable market intelligence data that would be extremely costly to acquire through traditional methods.

3 An interactive Internet site reduces the cost of communicating with clients, and can be kept more up to date than printed materials. Keeping customers informed and updated can be a high marketing expense if printed material is used. The Internet allows you to communicate with your client base faster, more effectively and cheaper than ever before. This provides greater added value for your customers as they are given a new means of keeping ahead of the game in learning about available products and services. It also dramatically improves the customer service that you can provide. However, this also enables you to communicate with your competitors faster, more effectively and cheaper than ever before. If you are looking for confidentiality then you need to review the business case for Extranets.

The business case for stage 3 – Internet representation

1 Ordering online can provide a huge potential reduction in sales costs. The Internet enables you to lead a client through the whole sales process and take the order without the involvement of a sales representative Although this is traditionally seen as an advantage for product-based companies, it can aid service providers as well in that it enables them to provide a demonstration of the service or indicate the level of expertise they offer. Again, customer service is improved and the perceived value of your Internet site is substantially increased.

2 You provide added value for the end client. Being able to place orders quickly and without the necessity of visiting a company outlet can provide a huge amount of added value for the end client. This allows you to sell to a wider potential national and international market, and maintain tighter controls over the process of order capture. For many organizations this creates a strong competitive advantage and greatly aids their market positioning.

3 Rationalization and cleaning up of internal processes and procedures. One of the strongest arguments for e-commerce (electronic commerce) is that it enables you to rationalize and clarify the way you do business. Through Internet representation you will face issues such as

international contract law and export legislation alongside the need to develop fast and foolproof systems.

In Figure 2.3 we outline the specific question each stage of development addresses and compare this with examples and benefits of implementation.

What is the business case for Extranets?

The business case for stage 1 – Extranet presentation

1 It provides a competitive advantage and creates loyalty. Mirroring the concept of a loyalty card, Extranets are being used to encourage a specific target audience to communicate with your organization. Users are given a password or even a dedicated phone number with log-in information. This gives them a sense of privilege. So long as this is supported by a strong and professional application with information that is relevant and regularly updated, an Extranet should prove to be a strong competitive positioning and a loyalty building initiative.

   This is as relevant for suppliers as it is for customers or prospects. Organizations can provide direct links for them to gain automatic orders and then negotiate down the price based on the reduction in administration. The increased communication links also increase supplier retention as they become more in tune with how you want to do business.

2 It reduces the cost of communicating with external organizations. The Internet enables you to communicate to external organizations faster, more effectively and cheaper than ever before. The main advantage here is that it does not enable this information to be accessed by competitors. Unlike printed material which can easily be obtained, access to an Extranet is harder to penetrate and involves your competitors actually obtaining the information illegally.

The business case for stage 2 – Extranet interaction

The arguments used to support the investment in an Internet Interaction are identical to the business case for Extranet Interaction initiatives except for three additional issues:

	What questions are you answering?	**Examples**	**Benefits**
Stage 1 Presentation	• Who are you? • Why are you credible?	• Company history • Annual report and accounts	• Strong corporate image • Credibility building • Market differentiation
	• What products and services do you sell?	• Catalogue, brochure	• Brand awareness • Global access to brochure • Customer education • Cross-selling opportunities
	• Why you? Your expertise/approach/ value for money etc. – your USP (unique selling proposition)	• Demonstration of expertise	• Persuasion
	• Why come back and visit us again?	• What's new? • Briefings/newsletters • New product updates • Special offers	• Fast and cost-effective customer update and communication
Stage 2 Interaction	• Why contact us?	• Easy response mechanisms	• Self-generating enquiry system
	• What product is best suited to my needs?	• Decision tree, taking the customer to the most appropriate product/service • Newsgroups/ conferences	• You obtain feedback as to what specific needs the client has
	• How can you solve some of my specific needs?	• Automatic responders • Email subscriptions • Online customer support • Complaint handling • Market research/ opinion • Voting mechanisms	• Automatic pre-qualification of enquiry • Advanced customer education • Cost-effective customer support • Filtering out of 'tyre kickers'
Stage 3 Representation	• How can I conduct business with your organization?	• Video/audio presentations of company and products • Integrated funnel into existing sales system • Online ordering or quotation system • Hybrid CD applications	• 90–100 per cent of the sale is conducted without involving a sales person • Added value to client • Rationalization of systems and procedures

Figure 2.3 Specific examples and benefits of Internet developments

1 Cost-effective market research and product testing. The advantage of Extranets is that they can enable you to have open, frank debates over product development and attitude surveys. They can be set up to be anonymous and open so that respondents can see previous discussions and either support or contradict other responses. You can move to a higher level of debate and the information produced contains more value.

You can test new product ideas out with suppliers prior to investing heavily with prototypes. You can gain an insight into costs before committing large resources.

2 Cost-effective support. Searchable databases have proved to be an extremely cost-effective route to support. This combined with a bulletin board and newsgroup can often reduce the need for a substantial in-house support team. The potential savings here are huge.

Many blue chip organizations are using Internet technology to downsize their customer or technical support functions. Done effectively, you can dramatically reduce costs and increase customer satisfaction.

3 Cost-effective promotional activity. Establishing the effectiveness of promotional activity can carry a high cost. Promotional literature needs to be created and tested. Direct marketing and database maintenance are crucial features. There also needs to be effective systems in place for monitoring the responses. Extranets have the capability of running daily promotions and offers with in-built delivery and monitoring. Organizations are just beginning to see and exploit this opportunity.

The business case for stage 3 – Extranet representation

The arguments used to support the investment in e-commerce outlined in the previous section are identical to the business case for Extranet Interaction initiatives. The main additional benefit for Extranets is that your competitors cannot openly explore your business processes. This is particularly pertinent if it exposes any weaknesses that you may have, e.g. stock availability, range of products, etc.

For suppliers and other business partners, Extranets can enable you to create closer and more efficient working relationships and automate the repetitive tasks within the relationship, e.g. order placement or repeat purchase. In Figure 2.4 we outline the specific question each stage of development addresses and compare this with examples and benefits of implementation.

	What questions are you answering?	**Examples**	**Benefits**
Stage 1 Presentation	• Would you like to see behind the front door? • Why should you stay loyal to our organization?	• Company policy • Business plan • News • Awards • Annual report and accounts • Demonstration of expertise	• Strong corporate image • Credibility building • Persuasion
	• What products and services do we sell and are looking to sell?	• Catalogue • Special offers • Product development plan	• Cross selling • Up selling • Consistent sales messages
	• Why come back and visit us again?	• What's new? • Briefings/newsletters • New product updates • Special offers	• Fast and cost-effective customer update and communication
Stage 2 Interaction	• Talk to us about our service	• Complaint handling • Market research/ opinion • Voting mechanisms	• High quality feedback • Cost-effective complaint handling
	• What can we do for you?	• Decision tree taking customer to the most appropriate product/service	• You obtain feedback as to what specific needs the client has
	• How can you solve some of my specific needs	• Newsgroups/ conferences • Automatic responders • Email subscriptions	• Cost-effective information provision • Consistent and easy communication
	• How can we help you further?	• Online customer support (sales or technical)	• Cost-effective customer support
Stage 3 Representation	• How can I conduct business with your organization?	• Direct links into back office systems • Integrated funnel into existing sales system • Online ordering or quotation system	• 90–100 per cent of traditional business communications is conducted online

Figure 2.4 Specific examples and benefits of Extranet developments for customers

	What questions are you answering?	Examples	Benefits
Stage 1 Presentation	• Would you like to see behind the front door? • Why should you stay loyal to our organization?	• Company policy • Contractual process • Our supplier policy • Awards • Annual report and accounts	• Credibility building • Persuasion • Corporate communication
	• How can you become more involved with us?	• Supplier needs • Product development plan	• Ease of communicating needs from suppliers
	• Why come back and visit us again?	• What's new? • Briefings/newsletters • New product updates • Special offers	• Fast and cost-effective supplier update and communication
Stage 2 Interaction	• Feedback what you can do for us • Changes in your prices	• Remote update to supplier records	• High quality supplier data because it is maintained by supplier
	• Apply for on-line tenders • Feedback what you think about us	• On-line tenders • Market research/ opinion • Voting mechanisms	• Fast tender response in electronic format • Feedback • Cost effective supplier complaint handling
	• Talk to us • Let us help you	• Newsgroups/ conferences • Online supplier support	• You obtain feedback as to what specific needs the supplier has • Cost-effective centralized communication • Quality supplier support
Stage 3 Representation	• How can ordering products and services from you be made electronically and automatically?	• Direct links into back office systems for EDI • Potential connection of customer direct to supplier • Automatic purchasing	• 90–100 per cent of traditional business communication is conducted online?

Figure 2.5 Specific examples and benefits of Extranet developments for suppliers

What is the business case for Intranets?

The business case for stage 1 – Intranet presentation

1 You can disseminate a consistent message more effectively than ever before. Speed of communication inside the organization is the key to competitive advantage. An Intranet can secure a consistent message sent instantly across the company, even to remote workers.
2 You can centralize all corporate communication in one arena, with huge savings in duplication and distribution costs. Paper is expensive and time-consuming. Intranets recover development costs usually within a matter of months.
3 The communication has the capacity to be higher quality. With animation, video, audio and strong use of graphics, communication can have a much stronger impact and therefore be more effective.

The business case for stage 2 – Intranet interaction

1 You are changing the culture of the organization in a controlled and managed way. You can diagnose employee attitude, provide a reaction and implement cultural change. Gaining a fast insight into what your employees think and feel about the organization is the starting point of any change process. The main benefits of Intranets have been in this arena.
2 People are visible and need spend less time internally marketing themselves. Many organizations could increase their productivity if they could create an environment where people spent less time communicating and more time doing. Intranets have enabled organizations to increase productivity rates by enabling an easy mechanism for people to market and communicate their projects and successes.
3 Everyone is 'singing from the same hymn sheet'. The key here is that people know where to go for information. It is centralized and people rely on the information because they are responsible for keeping it updated.

The business case for stage 3 – Intranet representation

1 Huge potential reduction in sales costs through remote working. This enables you to reduce overheads and optimize your use of sales personnel. Some companies have used this technology to create a virtual organization with no centralized office expenses.
2 Added value to end client. The sales person can conduct all administration and queries remotely, even within the client's premises. This speed to market will be critical to success in the twenty-first century.
3 Rationalization and cleaning up of internal processes and procedures. Interestingly, one of the strongest arguments for remote working is that it cleans up and rationalizes the way business is conducted.

In Figure 2.6 we outline the specific question each stage of development addresses and compare this with examples and benefits of implementation.

What next?

The outcome of using this model as part of the strategic decision-making process within the organization should be a planned Internet implementation strategy for the next five years. This will be founded on measurable objectives that can be easily and visibly monitored for review on a regular basis.

We now take each application of Internet technology, moving from this strategic perspective to the practical and technical issues. Each chapter has been designed with a senior manager in mind. We are not expecting you to gain a huge insight into the technology but we are aiming to provide in-depth coverage of the business opportunities and threats the application of this technology can bring you from a technical perspective.

Conclusion

This model is about movement across the three types of application of Internet technology. The issue is not about which box your organization should best leverage but the planned implementation of a route across the matrix.

	What questions are you answering?	Examples	Benefits
Stage 1 Presentation	• Who are we?	• Company history	• Reinforce the corporate image, message and mission
	• How are we doing?	• Annual report and accounts • Sales results	• Employee understanding and education
	• What products and services do we sell?	• Catalogue • Features and benefits	• Induction training • Remote access to product information for sales people • Pricing updates are instant
	• What makes us unique?	• Reviews • Press articles • Product features and benefits compared to industry • Consolidated market research information	• Communicate market positioning
	• What competitors do we have?	• Marketing information system • Competitor information	• Market awareness throughout organization
	• What's going on?	• What's new? • Briefings/newsletters • New product updates • Special offers/ promotions • Fun section	• Instant and consistent communication across the company
	• What systems and procedures do we use here?	• ISO9000/BS5750/IIP manuals • Forms to print off and fill in • Changes in procedures	• Cost-effective centralized procedure management
	• Who is using what in the organization?	• Meeting room availability • Car pool availability • Resource allocation	• Fast and easy management of scarce resources • Instant and consistent communication across the company
	• Who's who in the company? • What jobs are available?	• Telephone/email directory • CV and skills database • Job availability	• Ease of information access • Ease of induction training

Figure 2.6 Specific examples and benefits of Intranet developments (continued on pages 18–19)

	What questions are you answering?	**Examples**	**Benefits**
Stage 1 Presentation	• Who are our customers?	• Sales and marketing database read only • Overview of sales by industry, sales by company size, etc.	• Instant and consistent communication across the company about client details
Stage 2 Interaction	• What do people think about the company?	• Employee satisfaction questionnaires • Quality improvement suggestions	• Anonymous collection of employee attitudinal data and suggestions
	• How are we doing?	• Sales results with comments from sales people • Projected figures	• Direct news from the front-line
	• What products and services could we sell? • How can we improve our business?	• Product development suggestions	• Ideas from employees • Quality improvement suggestions
	• What are competitors doing?	• Business lost to competitors • Activity by competitors • Pricing updates	• Employees motivated to discover about the competition for themselves
	• What's going on?	• What's new from you? • Social events arranged • Fun section – gossip and things to buy and sell	• News desk which people can contribute to means a high usage rate
	• What can we do better?	• Suggestions for ISO9000/BS5750/IIP manuals • Online forms • Changes in procedures	• Quality systems implemented online throughout organization with instant publication
	• Where is everyone in the company? • What jobs are available?	• Networked diaries • CV and skills database with easy update for person outlined • Outline job application for internal vacancies	• Improved communication • Improved customer service

Figure 2.6 Specific examples and benefits of Intranet developments (*continued*)

	What questions are you answering?	Examples	Benefits
Stage 2 Interaction	• What is happening with our customers?	• Sales and marketing database with controlled update facility	• Instant and consistent communication across the company about client activity
Stage 3 Representation	• How can I work remotely?	• All software accessible from one centralized area with remote access • Video/audio presentations of company and products • Integrated funnel into existing sales system • Online ordering or quotation system/ hybrid CD applications	• People can perform all major elements of their jobs remotely. Offices used for face-to-face communications only

Figure 2.6 Specific examples and benefits of Intranet developments (*continued*)

The next chapters will address the three applications of the technology but each seek to demonstrate and illustrate the interaction and opportunities cross linking provides at a strategic level for your organization.

We seek to enable you to get it right first time so that you are faster to market and save the costs of redevelopment. This book is about enabling you to leapfrog your competitors and every section of this chapter will ensure you do just this.

On the Internet

Live on the Internet at: www.marketingnet.com/cyberstrategy/ we offer you:

- downloadable worksheets of this model so that you can start to fill in the benefits of each element of the matrix for your organization
- the ability to discuss your experience of the Internet with the authors and other readers of *Cyberstrategy*.

Chapter 3

Your Internet strategy

During the late 1980s, the Internet was hailed as the most revolutionary technology the computing industry had seen. However, it was not just the IT industry that would be affected by this communication revolution.

Corporations found that the Internet offered them new opportunities to communicate with their clients and their staff and the chance to access new audiences that other methods do not automatically reach. Marketing executives saw the chance to make new, direct contact with a target audience. Gradually the general public has also recognized the potential of fast, informal email communication and Internet resources in both their work and private lives. The growth potential seems endless, and it is now the task of managers and decision-makers to implement this ever changing technology in order to provide effective business solutions for both their clients and their organization.

Innovative companies were the first to explore the possibilities of Internet technology, developing early web sites and employing Internet-based applications within their organizations. In the general business population there was an initial distrust of the world wide web and the potential it could really offer in terms of business benefits and data control. This anxiety led to the majority of companies choosing to watch the innovators and wait to see where the new technology might take them.

The use of web technology still provokes some scepticism, but gradually the association of new media with international brand names, and their successful implementation of commercially viable web sites, Intranets and Extranet developments, has created a positive climate in which the benefits of this technology are well respected. The Internet is now accepted as a tool that can improve business efficiency.

To consolidate its position, the Internet must prove itself to be profitable and endure the same scrutiny afforded other business endeavours. No manager is going to implement a full-scale Internet project without proof that the results will justify the investment and that the business benefits are precisely what the company requires for its long-term development.

The Cyberstrategy Model can be used in the following ways by organizations looking to employ Internet technology:

- As a diagnostic tool to identify the business benefits your organization is seeking.
- As a method for discovering how your competitors are using the Internet.
- As a structure by which to segment and target your market.
- As a model to formulate an implementation plan that will achieve your aims.
- As a way of justifying your Internet project in the long term.
- As a means of determining who should be tasked with the development, and then the maintenance process.
- As a tool to assess how you will measure and ensure the success of your project.

This chapter aims to take you on a journey. It guides you through the decision-making process and determining whether Internet technology is a viable business proposition through to the practical task of entering your site in search engines which enables your target audience to find you on the Internet should you decide to go ahead.

Figure 3.1 gives you an overview of where the journey is leading. It also shows you the rationale behind the journey so that you can see what key questions we are answering on route.

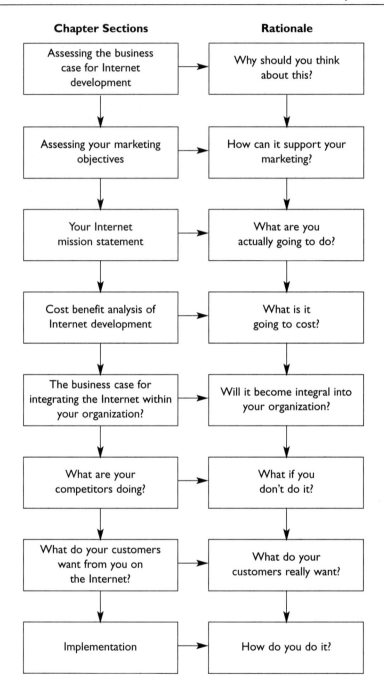

Figure 3.1   The structure flow diagram for Chapter 3

Assessing the business case

In order to plan your Internet presence, you need to review both the strengths and weaknesses of this new medium in terms of your business and communication needs.

Why should you think about this?

Whether you are an IT expert, or a marketing executive recognizing the value of Internet exposure, you face a difficult task in justifying the kind of investment needed to ensure that a web site will be a commercial success. Figure 3.2 outlines the major benefits of Internet development for a business organization. This diagram is designed to give you a sense of overview; each stage is examined in greater depth later.

So what is the Internet good for and where are the pitfalls?

Instant communication

The Internet is an ideal mechanism to communicate information about your organization, its products and services to a global audience. The increasing speed at which an organization has to adapt to its environment is poorly supported by print communication. Print (whether on paper or CD) delays publication because of the time it

	Benefits for business
Presentation stage	• Instant communication • Global communication • Cost savings for communicating with clients and staff • Corporate image adaptation • Corporate image development • Complementary communication channel • Passively attracting business interest
Interaction stage	• Receiving feedback from customers and potential clients • Test marketing potential
Representation stage	• Conducting business online

Figure 3.2 The business case

takes to reproduce and deliver materials. The Internet provides an instant form of communication.

This major benefit has been most appreciated by the IT industry. Decision-makers use the Internet as a virtual library and educational medium to keep up to speed with developments of new products as well as important issues affecting existing products. With online demos and ordering, the Internet has become the showcase and the delivery channel for IT products. This will ultimately have more of an impact as it is adopted by other industries.

The downside of this instant communication characteristic is that there are less quality standards in place. Because it is easy, fast and practically free (no reproduction or delivery costs), the quality is often affected and therefore there is a huge amount of material which is published with little or no attention to design, impact or quality of copy. In addition, published material is often allowed to decay. The pitfall of this is that information published on the Internet is seen as less reliable than information communicated in print. This perception is changing, particularly following a number of recent law cases where companies have been called to account for information that they have published on the Internet.

In summary, although the Internet is both fast and cost effective, it is not seen as a replacement for high quality printed communication about new products. For most organizations, it does not replace the need for a glossy brochure but can reduce the cost of reproduction as updates can be presented instantly online.

Global communication

Beyond speed, coverage is key to understanding how the Internet can support your organization. The Internet is the only telecommunications channel that can enable an organization to transmit a message universally across the world. Your organization has the ability to press one button and transmit one message uniformly to an international audience. Before this development, organizations relied on agents or distributors to extend the communication. This was often inefficient and expensive, and sometimes resulted in multiple messages being generated.

The potential of the Internet to generate export orders has been capitalized upon early in the US, especially for homogenous inter-

Nullifire

www.nullifire.com

Nullifire is an innovative intumescent paint manufacturer based in the UK. These paints are used to shield buildings as a passive protection against fire. Nullifire used the Internet as early as 1995 to promote their products world wide. They provided benefits and detailed specifications and received orders from China, Turkey and the Middle East. The orders came from potential distributors and, within a year of going live on the Internet, an additional five agents for their products had been established world wide. The cost comparison between using the Internet as a means of attracting agents and the alternative of visiting and meeting potential distributors meant that the Internet recouped its investment within a matter of months.

national products such as IT and music. This is becoming one of the key benefits of product promotion on the Internet. In our experience as an Internet marketing company, these benefits are more commonly appreciated by manufacturers seeking international orders and agents.

The key pitfall is that the Internet relies on individuals to search for information themselves, raising the issue of how added value can be emphasized online. This also raises the issue of how you can make it easy for potential clients to find your information, which we discuss later in this chapter.

Although the technology can be universally accessed across the world, language can be an interesting dilemma. Can messages that work in one geographical location be simply translated so that they will work in another? In traditional marketing, there is a wealth of evidence to support the need for localized communication that is tailored to the cultural, economical, social and political concerns of the target audience. Unfortunately, you do not have the luxury of being able to direct visitors from different countries to alternative versions of your information. So can you communicate powerfully across national boundaries?

Another pitfall is that you cannot restrict entry to your Internet

Courtaulds Fibres Viscose

www.courtaulds-viscose.com

Courtaulds Fibres Viscose, the leading European producer of speciality viscose fibre, faced precisely the language dilemma when they set up a web site aimed at spinners, weavers, knitters and garment manufacturers using their fibres in the UK, France and Germany. They needed to communicate fast and effectively in three different languages at the same time. The solution was to create a home page that offered each user the opportunity to access one of three different sites: an English, a French or a German site. All three were hosted and maintained in Britain, but each new article or feature was developed in three languages simultaneously.

This structure allowed Courtaulds to focus content on three distinct target audiences and provide information tailored for each country. This offered great flexibility, although producing each feature in a variety of languages was a time-consuming and more expensive process.

site based on geographic location. If you are an organization that only does business within one country, you cannot restrict entry from other countries except by creating an Extranet and instigating a registration process. This significantly affects manufacturers who wish to show pricing information distinct to individual geographical areas.

Cost of communication

Despite the frustrations of quality and global publication, organizations can see low cost as one of the most exciting opportunities of Internet technology. An Internet presence can be created for less than the price of a small direct mailshot. There are ongoing costs of keeping an Internet site live and the cost of updating the information must not be underestimated but the key is that there are relatively few production and distribution costs.

The reduction in the cost of communication is the major opportunity of the Internet. Most organizations that spend significant budgets achieving dynamic communication with their target audiences see this as the primary driving force for adopting Internet technology. Printers, publishers and repro-houses are already beginning to feel the impact of this aspect of the technology.

Corporate image adaptation

In traditional marketing, the focus is primarily directed at keeping a strong and consistent corporate image so as not to confuse the target audience. The thinking here is that, by maintaining a consistency, the product brand or image is being powerfully established and retained, and will therefore be more valuable. Brand capital is built through consistent messages constructed around the benefits of the product. The downside of this is that it can straitjacket the organization into only presenting one view of their brand/image.

The Internet allows organizations to legitimately step out of this straitjacket and communicate more informally (or off the record) with their target audiences. The Internet has become a great leveller in terms of communication style, with email pioneering the relaxed attitude that is prevalent online. Web sites provide the ideal vehicle to strike up an open communication link with your clients that is unconstrained by traditional business or publishing etiquette and rules. Through this you can show an exciting, dynamic and modern side to your company. Internet audiences are particularly receptive to this direct marketing approach.

This allows organizations to be seen in many contexts as talking more directly to the end customer. The advantages here are:

- Marketing efforts and their impact can be tested and verified before they are implemented elsewhere. All campaigns can be checked to see whether they produce a result online first.
- Product and service testing can be done discreetly with low risk to the organization as a whole. Products and services can even be launched on the Internet prior to full-scale production.
- Organizations can create undercurrents in the marketplace that will generate a demand and attract an audience with perceived added value before they are satisfied with supply.

Corporate image development

The other benefit associated with fast, cost-effective and global communication is that your organization can use the Internet to develop its image and establish its identity as unique. One of the most significant features of the Internet is that it is a superb levelling field and allows firms to compete head-on with any size of competitor. A professional online presence can convince a user of your credibility and reliability better than any other form of communication. Each company is constrained by the amount of graphics and design capability that the Internet can deliver, so everyone starts from the same position. This allows small companies to compete directly with their larger competitors and acquire valuable market share.

The Internet can be exploited to develop credibility by publishing case studies and testimonials of your past work, or simply by having a professional Internet presence that creates the image of a forward thinking and highly successful organization. With these tools you can begin to position such nebulous and intangible features as service and quality. You can therefore generate real market differentiation between your organization and others through this new communication medium. International brands can easily be established generating a homogenous image across the globe through multi-language and culturally oriented communication.

A complementary communication channel

The Internet has unique characteristics which complement and support traditional marketing efforts.

- The search capabilities of the Internet enable customers to find information relevant to them from a mass of product details, white papers, etc. The more complex the product the greater benefits to the organization tasked with presenting complicated information and the better the customer service delivered to the end client. Online catalogues are more user-friendly as a result of the Internet and have provided a high per order value spend as a result.
- The easy online booking and ordering nature of the Internet enables customers to take action instantaneously 24 hours a day. Here a

Grant Thornton International

www.gti.org

Grant Thornton International (GTI) is one of the world's leading networks of independent national firms providing audit, accounting, tax and specialist business advice to growing entrepreneurial businesses. GTI is represented in 93 countries and brings together more than 18 500 staff working in over 550 offices around the world.

GTI projects a consistent corporate image on all media. The organization decided to establish its own distinctive presence on the Internet which could relate to, and would bring together a number of diverse national web sites already online. The key objective was to produce a flexible design for the international site which firms could tailor for use in national sites.

A focus group from a sample of GTI firms helped to decide how the site should look. GTI's established corporate identity was applied and, in 1996, a design template was agreed and web site guidelines for member firms were produced.

Firms that had already generated sites, and those wishing to create a new presence on the Internet, agreed to conform to these guidelines and produce a home page that would mirror the newly designed GTI home page. Firms would, however, have a free rein on subsequent page design.

Email played a critical role in the communication and implementation of this decision. Offices were consulted and fully briefed on why investment in a global site identity would benefit the business in the long term. Such a strategy allowed firms to identify with, and become involved in, the development process. This facilitated the smooth acceptance of the new design.

What is crucial in this case study is the way in which new technology allowed fast and effective dialogue of international marketing communications strategy. Additionally, the decision was seen as collective rather than directed from one central source.

brochure can promote an easy call to action to take place online and also lower the cost of a call centre or internal response mechanism. Innovative training organizations use the Internet as the call to action on seminar or course promotions.

- The multimedia facilities of the Internet, although often restricted in many cases, enable you to present a fuller, more exciting presentation of your products and services. It is more closely aligned to TV than to print. An example of this is car manufacturers who provide 360° internal viewing/inspections of their vehicles.
- The provision of instant access to dynamic information is fast enabling the system to be used for first-level technical and product support. This is reducing the costs of such support whilst delivering an improved customer service facility. A popular example of this is Federal Express who have provided online tracking of parcel location for customers. This not only allowed the customers to have an easy lookup facility for their parcel, but enabled FedEx to significantly reduce their customer service functions.

The pitfalls are that the technology is still difficult for non-technical individuals to use and the speed is still not robust enough to support a true TV experience.

Passively attracting business interest

With traditional marketing media, the responsibility lies with your organization to communicate out to the marketplace. Emphasis is given to direct mailing target audiences that have been selected as appropriate for each project. The Internet offers the unique opportunity for you to passively market, enabling prospective clients to search you out via an international medium and select the product or service that best suits their needs. Effectively you have a virtual sales person at work 24 hours a day who can internationally respond to clients' needs and inquiries remotely. This is a major benefit for organizations with limited marketing or sales resources.

The pitfalls of this are that you cannot target the benefits of your products and services to a particular audience as accurately as with printed materials. In print you have control of where the material is sent or seen. Therefore the secret here is to set up a filter system where specific target audiences select different paths within the Internet site. You then have the ability to position the benefits accordingly.

Receive feedback from clients and potential clients

All day, every day you can obtain valuable client feedback via your Internet site. A virtual sales person can lead a client through the decision-making process to direct them towards one of your products or services, providing you with an understanding of that client's needs and desires. You are acquiring pre-qualified and well-documented sales leads that are more likely to result in genuine orders. This filtering system is not possible in any other medium.

This also provides an invaluable opportunity to develop customer service and generate increased customer satisfaction and loyalty. If you receive a complaint either from your site or through email you have the ability to respond immediately and demonstrate how committed your organization is to customer care.

Test marketing

The Internet also offers your organization the opportunity to access an audience for test marketing purposes. New products or developments can be tested via your online community to gauge how the market will react before any significant investment is made.

Conducting business online

The strongest justification for Internet investment is the ability to generate online orders. You can effectively build a virtual shop front. This has to be the greatest benefit of the Internet but is most appropriate for organizations marketing products that can be quickly and easily distributed to the end client post-order.

Summary

The amount of budget, time and resources allocated to your Internet project is dependent on how important the above issues are to your organization. We recommend that these are quantified even at this early stage.

In this section we have used the Cyberstrategy Model to look at Internet technology from a total business perspective, in particular looking at how a company benefits from using Internet technology.

However, the majority of Internet applications are generated for an organization to present itself to the general public. There is much dispute as to whether this medium is advertising, PR, passive direct mail, etc. In reality it is a new marketing medium and therefore the next task is to identify how Internet technology fits in with your marketing goals.

Assessing your marketing objectives

How can it support your marketing?

Figure 3.3 assesses the marketing benefits offered by each stage of Internet development.

By establishing three separate stages of Internet development, the model will help you to conceptualize a detailed match between your existing marketing strategy and the potential benefits offered by Internet technology. The model can then be used to help formulate a structured marketing plan designed to roll out a specific Internet application for your organization that will use the most appropriate skills set and ensure that you achieve the long-term marketing aims you have identified.

To conclude, you might set out your marketing objectives as in Figure 3.4.

Your Internet mission statement

Where are you actually going?

To manage the integration of new technology it is useful to generate a document detailing the core purpose of the organization and why it is using the Internet. This might be called the mission or 'vision' statement of the Internet site.

This is important because it sets out the *raison d'être* of the site in tune with the *raison d'être* of the organization. This enables your end client to immediately differentiate whether you are what they are looking for. It also gives them a focus for exploring your site further. The statement can be introduced as a working document that will

Stages: Issues	Marketing objective to:
Presentation: • Your brand needs to reach a wider audience, or needs to develop as a more homogenous identity. • Your company needs to emphasize the success of what it does and develop a reliable image. • You want to stress your USP (unique selling proposition) in relation to your competitors. • You want to reach more people: clients and distributors. • You want to communicate faster and better with your clients.	• Build a strong corporate image and identity. • Increase brand awareness. • Increase corporate reputation and credibility. • Increase market differentiation. • Provide global access to your brochure. • Educate your customers. • Access new cross-selling opportunities. • Persuade users to consider your organization. • Generate a fast and cost-effective customer update and communication system.
Interaction: • You want a targeted and meaningful dialogue with your end client where you obtain as much information about them as they do about you.	• Create inherent added value and repeated calls to action or decision points to effectively create a self-generating enquiry system. • Obtain feedback as to what specific needs the client has. • Gain automatic pre-qualification of enquiry. • Educate the end customer. • Offer cost-effective customer support. • Filter out time wasters.
Representation: • Complete transactional sales process from enquiry through to order.	• 90–100 per cent of the sale is conducted without involving a sales person. • Provide added value to client. • Rationalize systems and procedures

Figure 3.3 Specific marketing objectives of corporate Internet development

Stages: Issues	Marketing objective to:
Presentation	• Increase awareness of our brand by 20 per cent. • Develop our corporate image and create a unified image of our organization for our clients and employees. • Establish the credibility of our company in providing X. • Educate our customers, and potential customers in how to purchase effectively from us and take them through key decision criteria. • Provide global access to our brochure and reduce distribution and print costs. • Associate our company with new media.
Interaction	As above, plus: • Generate qualified inquiries of 5 per cent of total lead generation. • Improve our customer service by offering 24-hour turnaround on queries. • Create a dialogue with our clients and potential clients – obtain 10 product ideas yearly. • Acquire marketing information about our client and potential client needs and desires – saving X on research expenditure.
Representation	As above, plus: • Generate orders and increase our annual turnover by 5 per cent.

Figure 3.4 Example of specific marketing objectives for Internet development

act as a general guide for the project, ensuring that everyone involved is aiming for the same end result.

Overleaf is an example of a vision statement prepared by a manufacturing firm. This business relied heavily on research and the development of new products to ensure that it stayed ahead of its competitors and provided the best products for its international network of distributors. The process began with an outline of the primary business aims:

> Our Internet site improves the services we provide for our international distributor network. Each distributor needs to know about our latest research and development and have access to details of new products before they appear on the market. We would also like to involve them in product development and the test marketing of new concepts.

The initial statement was clear in its aims, but through discussion was honed to include more specific details:

> In three years time we want to be using Internet technology to provide an instant two-way communication service for our international distributor network. Each distributor will be informed of our latest research and development, and details of all new products will be provided (including data, graphics, special features and a pricing guide) before they appear on the market. We will involve distributors in product development and the test marketing of new concepts.

This second statement was accepted as a confident assertion of a business vision, providing all employees with a time framework and a clear idea of what should be achieved within three years.

Cost-benefit analysis of Internet development

Once you have identified the overall business case, your marketing objectives and the mission statement for the site, you can then start to produce a detailed cost benefit analysis to justify the investment. In print media it is relatively easy to establish how many people will see a particular newspaper or magazine advert. In television advertising viewing figures are predicted and accepted as justification of the price of advertising space. In web marketing, however, little proof can be provided as to how many people have seen your site, or have become interested in your company as a result.

However well planned your Internet development is, it will still be

What is it going to cost?

Stage and marketing objective	Characteristic of the Internet	Potential cost savings	Potential long-term revenue generation
Presentation *Increasing brand image*	Instant communication	10 per cent reduction in newsletter/catalogue print and distribution	Customer loyalty and retention increases by 5 per cent
	Global communication	3 per cent cost saving in international brochure and newsletter production and distribution	Ability to attract international agents and distributors Orders in the region of 1 per cent of turnover
	Cost of communication	Further 1 per cent reduction in the costs of brochure and newsletter production and distribution	
	Corporate image adaptation	Ability to test market new campaigns: 10 per cent reduction in test marketing costs	Ability to reach market segments with an adapted image
	An additional and complementary communication channel	• Multimedia can reduce the sales qualifying stage • Online booking reduces the order processing resources within the organization • Cost reduction in technical manual production 50 per cent • Reduction in technical support resources 20 per cent	Improved customer service providing a competitive edge
Interaction *Creating a self-generating leads system*	Passively attracting business interest	Reduction in costs of qualifying leads	5 per cent of enquiries generated from the Internet
Representation *Providing another channel to market*	Conducting business online	50 per cent decrease in order handling costs	5 per cent of orders through the Internet

Figure 3.5 Example of cost benefit analysis of corporate Internet development

necessary to justify in real terms the investment each stage will demand. Figure 3.5 provides an example of how these cost savings can be quantified over a three-year time frame. This worksheet provides you with the ability to quantify the business benefits of each stage of Internet development.

The Cyberstrategy Model provides a framework for looking in detail at the motives, costs and benefits for every stage of Internet development. By using the model to assess your organization, you will be able to formulate a well thought out business case for producing an Internet site.

However, it is important to remember that there are ongoing maintenance costs associated with a web site, so it should be seen as a long-term investment that will require numerous revisits and assessments over a number of years. In addition to the costs of updating the web site so that it shows a true and accurate presentation of your organization, it is also important to address the issue of how the Internet will be integrated within the organization. You must ensure that updates to the site are a natural extension of your traditional marketing activities and that the handling of output is seamless.

We recommend that at the same time as justifying the Internet as a promotional tool for the organization, there should be an assessment of its internal use and adoption throughout the organization.

The business case for integrating the Internet within your organization

The Internet can support many of the critical core activities of any business or organization. Therefore, the key question is what added value will it bring within the organization that will justify the change process of implementing an intuitive and natural internal development.

Will it become integral into your organization?

To answer this, we recommend the use of Porter's Value Chain Analysis. We highlight the business case of adopting Internet technology as a business tool within your organization. Michael E. Porter asserts that a firm's competitive advantage is generated through a variety of component functions that make up the structure of the organization as a whole. Activities are divided into primary and supporting areas, all of which have the

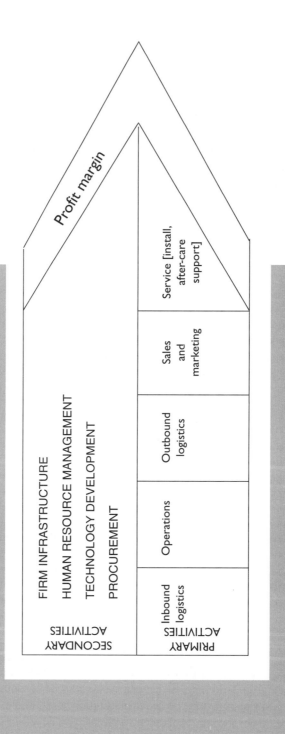

Figure 3.6 Porter's generic value chain

potential to be influenced by an Internet development. Figure 3.6 expands Porter's Generic Value Chain, adding the Internet to the activities he identifies.

The corporate Internet development sits around Porter's model as an external tool that can support all internal activities and increase the overall margin and competitive advantage, which is what Porter assumes that every firm is striving towards. The Internet therefore functions as a supporting agent for the elements that contribute to the long-term business success of the company.

How critical this new technology is to your company will largely depend on how close a match you can make between the advantages it offers Porter's defined activities and the advantage your company is seeking.

Porter's model looks primarily at the existing activities of an organization, providing a structure by which the performance of a firm can be critically assessed. By adding an Internet element to the diagram, we would suggest that it is taken as an assessment of the potential your company has in each activity to make improvements and increase your margin and competitive advantage in the long term. The Internet can be seen as a tool that can sustain and enhance the success of each area and the way in which a company differentiates itself from its competitors.

How the Internet influences different regions of Porter's model varies from activity to activity.

Primary activities

Inbound logistics

Inbound logistics cover the interaction between the organization and its suppliers. The need for 'just in time' provisions has led to increased need for instant communication between suppliers and supplied at all stages of the manufacturing chain.

- **Email.** Email and the Internet allow manufacturers and their suppliers the opportunity to communicate in a unique and instant way. Email provides the additional benefit that it is self-documenting and therefore automatically creates a route for tracing back orders and responses.

  This automatically cleans up and simplifies the supply process as the need for bits of paper is alleviated and decisions can be put into action quickly and easily. It might be argued that the overall effect is similar to that of a phone call, but email also enables multiple supplier communication to be automated and huge time efficiencies to be made.

- **Browser access.** Supplier and potential supplier sites on the Internet offer your organization further education about how to best procure items. Just as you aim to educate your customers as to the most effective way of buying, so will your suppliers. Many organizations choose suppliers for subjective reasons (they were recommended, they are local, they are friends of the chairman, etc.), but a facility that offers an objective view of the supplier's marketplace and sees them in a wider context can be extremely powerful.

- **Newsgroups.** In terms of service industries, inbound logistics tend to mean the exchange of knowledge between parties. The Internet can have a dramatic impact through this mechanism as ideas are posted live on the web so that people throughout the world can access them. Never has the exchange of intellectual property been so easy, particularly with interactive sites where replies can be added to a bulletin board.

    Specifically in terms of sourcing, newsgroups can not only provide a mechanism to post tender documents in the public domain, but also to assess others' responses to certain products.

    Consultancy and advice is another area where newsgroups can be helpful. It is fascinating to see what intellectual property is given away in these areas which in other circumstances would be a chargeable service.

Operations

- **Email.** The Internet has the power to influence the operational capabilities of an organization by providing an easy response and communication mechanism. Internal email between customers, front-end staff and operations people can significantly increase production efficiencies and lead to a reduction in the sales cycle.

    With consultancy companies, there is a clearer link between the potential of the Internet and the operations of their business as advice and reports can be delivered via email or an Internet site. Similarly, online recruitment agencies can perform most of their functions over the Internet, advertising jobs and accepting applications via the net, organizing a personal interview after the CV has been checked and approved. Here we are not talking about the use of an Internet site, merely the use of email as an internal business resource.

- **Browser access.** The business case for enabling operations people to have direct access to browser access to the Internet is less obvious. It is particularly pertinent in fast-moving industries where the operations personnel need up to the minute information about changes, e.g. technology, products affected by international law or exchange rates, etc. The key question here is will the Internet enable our operations people to make products which are better or cheaper? Often the answer is no, unless the product is intellectual property where the Internet provides access to information which maintains this knowledge.
- **Newsgroups.** The business case for enabling operations people to have direct access to newsgroups is their education can be facilitated. For example, in a manufacturing environment, there are newsgroups about how to repair and maintain equipment. These newsgroups provide information that even the manufacturer may not know about. In a service environment, newsgroups can be used to maintain knowledge bases or current levels of expertise. Knowledge workers use newsgroups to post questions and build a support network of contacts and specialist networks that enhance their service offering.

Outbound logistics

- **Email.** The Internet has the power to influence the outbound capabilities of an organization by enabling the product to be delivered electronically. Consultancy and the sale of intellectual property are the major examples of how a product might be delivered via Internet technology. For many UK companies, this has meant the ability to work internationally where before the speed of delivery through postal methods meant that they could not compete.

  Software manufacturers can also use the Internet to deliver their product, generating packages that will function over the Internet or are just transported via the technology. For other industries the Internet can provide an ideal mechanism for communicating with distribution channels and ensuring that all elements are functioning in tandem and with the greatest efficiency. This can again consolidate and rationalize internal structures and provide a slicker service all round.

  Customer support can be provided internationally for the same price as nationally specific. This enables you to expand your market globally just through the introduction of Internet technology within the organization.
- **Browser access.** The Internet can be used to recruit new distributors or agents for your services, new organizations to network with. A

search can be made online for organizations fitting specific criteria. They can then be emailed with an invite and discussions started. Once a relationship is built, the use of Internet technology can be the core channel of communication. When you compare this route with the costs involved in going overseas and finding a new agent, the costs are less than negligible.

- **Newsgroups.** These can be used to broadcast the need for a new agent in a specific country and again as described above provides significant cost savings.

Sales and marketing

- **Email.** We have already detailed how the Internet is used successfully as a marketing tool, providing an extra communication channel with customers and between businesses throughout the world. The use of Internet technology within the organization also provides an exceptionally cheap customer communication channel. Direct email shots to your whole client base is a fraction of the cost of one direct mailshot campaign to a single customer.
- **Browser access.** The Internet can also provide important online information resources for sales executives to use in the field to prospect new customers. The Internet can be used within a sales team as a valuable resource to access information about competitors and market developments to ensure that they stay ahead of the industry and can provide the most informed advice for their contacts. All of this will improve customer service by up-skilling the professionalism of the sales effort.
- **Newsgroups.** Sales people who are adept at using newsgroups have found them to be exciting meeting areas to network with potential clients. They are deliberately designed to be non-commercial and you will still often find a strong reaction against actively promoting either yourself or your organization within these areas. However, they are a useful place to identify key prospects where individuals disclose issues their organizations are faced with.

Service

- **Email.** The service potential of the Internet and email is one of the most exciting realms of the Internet for organizations where long-term, successful, relationships with clients provide the backbone of their business. Clients can leave queries or complaints for customer service teams to respond to, rather than phoning the company and, often after being held in a frustrating telephone queue, explaining themselves to someone at the other end. The potential for conflict is reduced when complaints are made through email and a considered and lengthy response can be given after the team has had time to follow up the problem. This has immeasurable value for all firms where customer satisfaction is important, and will reduce the number of lost clients for any organization which generates and maintains a successful system. Again the hidden benefit of asking for email complaints or queries is that they are self-documenting in electronic format for easy storage and retrieval for further analysis.

This also holds true for your service to your suppliers and distributors, and employees. If you create a system in which communication is open and easy, relationships are improved and you will begin to learn from all the areas of your business.

- **Browser access.** The Internet can be used to up-skill service and technical support staff on the issues that affect your market and your business. Can you put a price on the reassurance factor that your front-line staff are in tune with your market place and your competition? Many organizations fear that their staff will use the Internet as a recreational toy rather than as a professional resource, but this argument can be easily counteracted by monitoring and filtering access only to a selected list of key sites which will add to their effectiveness. There are many different approaches to creating these filters and monitors.
- **Newsgroups.** For service staff with a problem solving a customer query, newsgroups to your suppliers can be extremely powerful but this is only relevant when you are in a distributor role and the manufacturer supports this facility. In most other cases, newsgroups can be extremely time-consuming with little direct benefits.

Summary

The main business case for integrating Internet technology can be found in supporting the primary activities of your business. We recommend that you plot your perceived benefits on a grid – see Figure 3.7 as an example.

If the business case is still not strong enough to support the integration of the Internet, we recommend that you look at the secondary activities in addition as below.

Level of internal integration with the Internet	Inbound logistics	Operations	Outbound logistics	Sales and marketing	Service
Implementation of email	Fast supplier contact which is self-documenting and consistent	Faster communication with client and sales personnel	Delivery of report, product or software to end client	Direct, easy and cheap communication channel to customers	Direct communication channel to customers
Implementation of Internet access through a browser	Identifying the best methods of product sourcing	Increases the knowledge-based element of the product by access to online knowledge sources	Used to search for potential new distribution agents or channel	Good prospecting system. Effective and cost-effective resource to upskill sales team on the market competitors	Easy access to competitor and market information
Access to newsgroups on the Internet	Widening our tendering process and obtaining free advice	Maintenance of operational expertise and equipment	Used to search for potential new distribution agents or channel	Good prospecting system and opportunity for sales people to network	Access to newsgroups to aid with solving customer queries

Figure 3.7 Example assessment of the business case for integrating Internet technology within your primary activities

Secondary activities

Infrastructure

Email alone can be a superb starting point to any Intranet or Extranet development and, it can be argued, forms the basis and foundation of their success. Setting up company-wide email must be seen as an infrastructure cost and therefore just like a telephone system is almost a cost of doing business in the twenty-first century. In addition early adoption of corporate-wide Internet access and email must be seen in the longer-term perspective for taking hold of the benefits which Extranets and Intranets can offer.

Human resource management

The Internet can be used as an effective recruitment tool, particularly in attracting computer-literate individuals. Recruitment companies can be sourced through the Internet and all dealings with them made electronically. Alternatively, job adverts can ask for CVs to be sent electronically which makes the process of assessment and filtering not only easier but also less costly.

Training organizations and HR suppliers are already well profiled on the Internet and a significant percentage of products are available for testing and demonstration online. You can even request potential or existing employees to conduct personality profile testing live and have the results recorded and then emailed to you. Again professional up-skilling of HR personnel is another key benefit the Internet can bring to your organization. Government legislation, health and safety advice and other legislative matters are all covered extensively on the Internet.

Technology development

In a similar way to infrastructure, the cost of keeping up to date with technology now includes the cost of having Internet access and the time resources to allocate to it.

Information about technology advances are given on the Internet and the delay in online and printed publication can be longer than your organization can afford. Very few organizations can afford the luxury of not keeping up with changes in the marketplace and with technology.

Procurement

The Internet is an ideal tool for sourcing suppliers. Some suppliers will take orders via the web and offer you valuable customer service facilities online. This can all speed up the procurement process and provide you with access to information resources hitherto difficult to acquire.

At this point, you will have identified the business case for externally promoting and internally integrating the Internet within your organization. However, any recommendations you make cannot be put forward without due consideration to your competitors. At one extreme, you may be pushing your organization to innovate ahead of everyone and bearing unnecessary costs which may not be justified later. At the other extreme, you may think you are being radical and strategic but in fact you are lagging behind your competitors and as a result have no associated benefits as the Internet has become the cost of doing business in your industry.

What are your competitors doing?

What if you
don't do it?

Another use for the Cyberstrategy Model is as a diagnostic tool to assess what your competitors are doing online. This exercise will provide you with some benchmark examples and demonstrate how similar organizations have succeeded or failed in this new marketing dimension. This kind of knowledge will help you to adopt Internet technology in the most appropriate and successful way.

A primary use of the Internet is as a research tool. Online information sources are one of the best ways for you to get to know how your industry and competitors are using the Internet to achieve different business aims. To reach your competitors' web sites, search for their company name or use some keywords that are pertinent to your business in one of the many search engines available online.

Take a look at any sites listed, noting down the kind of facilities they provide (for example, search, ordering, response forms, private forums or chat rooms, etc.). Notice how graphics, animation and information are presented, and the effect it has on you as a user. Getting to know which sites you like and dislike using will help you formulate an initial idea of what your own site should offer.

As an example, we have taken a fictional flower distribution industry and compared the way the Internet is used by two high street brands with a company who does business solely via the Internet. We begin by mapping each firm on the Cyberstrategy Model (see Figure 3.8).

Presentation

Flower Centre produced a site designed entirely to entice people to visit their shops around the UK. They had already established themselves as a brand name through a network of high street outlets, and secured 50 per cent of the market in terms of bouquet deliveries and off the shelf cut flowers. They saw no need to develop online ordering, but chose to focus on the personal service they could provide by customers visiting their shops, or phoning a specific outlet. Their corporate site strove to develop the credibility and reliability of their brand. Case studies of satisfied customers and profiles of individual

Stage	Company
Presentation	Flower Centre
Interaction	Flower Power
Representation	Blooms Direct

Figure 3.8 Competitors mapped on Cyberstrategy Model

employees and their work were regularly updated, and aimed to offer users entertaining anecdotes of how Flower Centre had helped to create the ideal birthday, wedding, etc. Different festival days throughout the year were given particular attention, always suggesting that your local Flower Centre could take care of Mother's Day or a special occasion for you. A 'shop finder' also helped users quickly locate the nearest Flower Centre to their home, and maps and details were provided to make any contact as easy as possible – even the names of the people who would answer the phone were listed!

Interaction

Flower Power wanted to establish more rapport and direct contact with their clients. This innovative firm provided competitions and lots of response forms for users to reply to specific requests, like that for the best message to accompany a Valentine's bouquet, or tell Flower Power what their favourite flowers were. This provided invaluable marketing information that would have been difficult to obtain through traditional methods, and encouraged people to visit Flower Power outlets around the country and learn about this new, customer-friendly brand name. Even though Flower Power had less than half the number of high street stores as Flower Centre, they soon became a sought-after brand with a reputation for taking an interest in their clients and producing out of the ordinary, individualized bouquets.

Stage	How competitors use the Internet
Presentation	● Stressing and establishing the brand name. ● Developing the corporate image. ● Developing credibility to generate desire in the user to visit high street outlet.
Interaction	As above, plus: ● Trying to elicit inquiries and request personal information about users (response forms). ● Inviting users to make comments and voice their needs and desires. ● Generating a dialogue. ● Adding value for the user (competitions). ● Still aimed at persuading the user to visit an off-line outlet to make a purchase.
Representation	● Encouraging online ordering (exclusive online discounts, ease of use, good product photographs, etc.) ● Less focus on gaining insight into what clients want.

Figure 3.9　How competitors have exploited the Internet

Representation

Blooms Direct developed a very different Internet site. They had no high street stores at all, but conducted all their business over the Internet. Therefore, this site was packed with photographs of the different bouquets the firm could provide, each page offering the user the opportunity to order the product immediately via the web. This approach resulted in a weaker focus on gaining customer data through response forms and requests for personal information, and a much stronger push to make a sale while the user was within the site.

The methods each competitor used are shown in Figure 3.9 and the benefits summarized.

These examples help to demonstrate how you can select the most appropriate Internet strategy for your organization, based on your long-term objectives. If you apply this diagnostic model to your own industry, you should also be able to identify where your company lies, or might potentially lie on the grid. It will also encourage you to assess critically what your major competitors are doing online. This will help you formulate a strategy to take your organization to the area of the grid where your individual business goals can be achieved, and where you can compete effectively with the rest of your industry.

Having done all this preparation you are still left with the ultimate and most important question of all: what do your customers want from you on the Internet?

What do your customers want from you on the Internet?

When you begin to develop your Internet presence it will help to have as many different ideas of what features you might incorporate and how the site will look before you start. Particularly in the first few months online, it will be beneficial to include some features that you know your target audience will want: some 'quick wins' to get the site up and running. The only way of being sure that you will get this right first time is to ask clients what they would like and value in a web site. For many organizations market research at this early stage also provides the first indication of how many people within their target market use the Internet on a regular basis and are likely to see their web site. This kind of information will clearly have strategic implications in determining the scale of their Internet development.

> What do your customers really want?

It is important that your organization considers its options, if the market research you complete demonstrates that few of your clients actually use the Internet. Making a long-term investment in a medium that few of your target audience will see could prove to be an expensive project that will yield little or no return for a significant period of time. However, by getting involved early, you will prepare yourself and your company for the time when your customers catch up and begin to use the Internet.

The most important group to consult are the people you want to attract to your site. Many companies feel that they know their customers and give them what they want and like and are tempted to research only prospects. Others just research prospects and then produce sites which actually turn off their existing clients.

The Internet is a new medium, and sometimes what clients want

Warwick Business School: The benefits of market research

www.wbs.warwick.ac.uk

Warwick Business School began the development of their Internet presence with one goal in mind: to attract potential MBA students to choose Warwick. It was agreed by the team heading the project that to attract Internet-using professionals, technology should be fully employed to indicate that Warwick was at the forefront of new media, and was therefore one of the most exciting and forward-thinking places to study. To achieve this it was decided that a 'virtual lecture' should be available online for users to experience what it was like to study at Warwick. A panoramic view of the lecture theatre would be provided, and supported with an audio sample of a lecture. Existing MBA students were extremely excited about this possibility.

Before this idea was put into practice, Warwick Business School commissioned a brief research study in which potential MBA students were asked what single thing the School could provide online that would persuade them to select Warwick. And the answer? One sheet of A4 text that someone could print out and hand to their manager highlighting the price of an MBA and the business justification for why the investment was worthwhile. This solution achieved the same results, but was a lot less time-consuming, less expensive and much easier to maintain and keep up to date.

online can be very different to what they want under normal circumstances. In addition to this, the problem with researching prospective clients is that you have to explain your business in depth before starting to investigate what value you can provide them online. In our experience, this often results in lower quality responses. Our recommendation is to research all the target groups you are looking to satisfy online.

The example of Warwick Business School stresses the need for qualification of the features your clients want from your web site. If they want freebies, or detailed data sheets, then try to provide them. Similarly if they don't appreciate animated graphics and games, then don't spend extra time and money creating them. You will only attract a certain kind of user, but at the end of the day you will receive inquiries that are pre-qualified and access contact details for people who are likely to want your products and services.

It is important to accept from the outset that it makes sense to aim for the best quality of visitors to your site (i.e. people who are most likely to purchase your products or services), rather than hope for a vast number of hits. This may seem obvious, but promised high hit rates can occlude your view of how the site will actually generate revenue and a return for your investment. Your web site will only actively produce business rewards through enquiries, a greater awareness of your company and through actual orders.

Interview methods

Telephone interviews can be an effective way of discovering what kinds of features different people are looking for, and will help you become more aware of precisely who your online audience is. The telephone offers the opportunity for fast, low cost, one-to-one communication, and the chance to get into a real dialogue with the people who will one day use the Internet site you develop. Some drawbacks of telephone interviews are that they must be kept brief, difficult to use visual aids and do not always establish the credentials of the interviewee. However, taken as a starting point in the development of a corporate web site, they can prove illuminating and be instrumental in devising a site that will achieve your aims, and satisfy your target market first time.

Alternative ways of acquiring opinion might be via a postal survey. By posting information, visual items can be included, and the respondent has the freedom to complete the questions in their own time. The post is also relatively cheap and people will often be more willing to respond anonymously to personal questions. However, many questionnaires will not be returned, a covering letter needs to be carefully worded to successfully elicit a response and the questions must be set in as simple a way as possible. Written questionnaires offer less flexibility than face-to-face contact and answers have to be accepted by a study even if they are vague or misunderstood.

Email surveys have the same advantages and disadvantages as postal surveys, especially today when most email users are wise to 'junk' mail, and tend not to respond to anything resembling them. Email does, however, offer many users a more informal way of responding than posted questionnaires. You can also be sure that you are talking to individuals who understand and are used to Internet technology and should therefore obtain some detailed and meaningful responses.

Personal interviews can offer the most flexible opportunity to find out what the interviewee really thinks and wants, but are extremely time consuming and expensive to conduct.

Questionnaires

Figure 3.10 is an example questionnaire designed for a telephone survey. It aims to establish some basic facts: what does the interviewee think of the company in question, do they use the Internet, etc.? We have included many more questions than we would normally use in one interview to give you a better idea of the kinds of things you might ask. It is important to keep each interview short, concluded in a positive manner and no-one is inconvenienced.

The aim of such a short interview should be to generate a natural dialogue and encourage the interviewee to chat as freely as possible.

Introduce your company and explain that you are calling to discuss a new Internet development, using terms that the interviewee is likely to recognize and understand. Ask the interviewee if they could spare some time to answer some brief questions.

By generating a conversation based around questions such as these, you will be able to gauge how your clients feel about your planned Internet project, and begin to assess what kind of features to provide for them online.

It is also useful to take this opportunity to discover how generally happy your customers are with the service that you provide. In identifying any weaknesses now, you will be able to exploit the customer service potential of the Internet and actively target any client dissatisfaction through this new medium. Such an exciting new development can also act as an ideal vehicle for making contact, and then keeping in touch with your clients.

For potential or desired clients, the questions can be amended, and the interviewer should be prepared to provide background information about your company and the services you offer. Answers to this survey will probably be less detailed, but will also help to formulate an idea of what kind of features will work well online.

Internet user	Non internet user
1 Would you use the Internet to search for a supplier?	1 What services/ information could a firm like X provide that you would like regular access to, and might consider going onto the Internet to get?
2 If you were searching for a firm like X on the Internet, what keywords would you use?	2 What services provided by X do you most appreciate and value?
3 Would having fast and easy email contact with X be beneficial to you?	3 Would having fast and easy contact with X be beneficial to you?
4 What services/information could a firm like X give you regular and easy access to, and might persuade you to visit their site on a regular basis?	4 Might you consider using the Internet or email in the future? If not, why?
5 What sites do you go to first on the Internet and why?	5 What features or services might persuade you to use X rather than an alternative X company?
6 What features or services might persuade you to use X rather than an alternative X company?	6 What is your most important consideration when selecting a company like X?
7 What is your most important consideration when selecting a company like X?	7 What kind of information could X provide that might help you when dealing with your staff or customers?
8 What do you like and value most about X?	8 Is there anything X could do to improve its service to you?
9 What kind of information could X provide that might help you when dealing with your staff or customers?	9 What keywords spring to mind when you think of X or a company like them?

Figure 3.10 Example market research survey

Implementation

How do you do it?

At this stage in the book, you are probably at a point where you have created a business case which looks at every angle and you are now desperate to cut to the quick and suggest the route to implementation. The next section of the book takes you through a detailed checklist for issues to address.

Domain names

Your online brand may be as crucial to your corporate image as your offline name. Making certain that you can be known by the same name on the Internet and off it will be vital in terms of establishing a homogenous brand identity throughout your marketing mix. Everyone must know where to find you online and, as most people search for a known company by typing their name in as part of a web address, the more intuitive and obvious your domain name is the better.

You have the choice of selecting an international address, i.e. .com, e.g. yourcompany.com or a country-specific address such as .co.uk or .fr (France), .se (Sweden) and so on.

The domain name you choose will depend primarily on how international your business activities are, or are likely to be in the future. A .com name indicates that the company is an international name, this is also used in the US which means that you might be mistaken for an American organization. A .co.uk address suggests that the organization is UK based.

We would suggest that you consider securing both the international and national version of your brand name to ensure that no-one else can trade online with your name. We have had a number of instances where an Internet site has achieved a wonderful success under an international domain name and a competitor has taken the national equivalent of the name and gained a head start because of this. Passing-off actions can only happen if they are using your company name or a trademark but the legal world is still catching up with the Internet and the lines can often be difficult to define (see Appendix). In any case the investment is relatively small and will make certain that your brand and identity is protected within this new marketplace.

Gain internal commitment

Another important group to consult is your employees. They will need to be ambassadors of your Internet development if they are to support its implementation and contribute to its success. Your staff can be a valuable walking and talking advertisement for your web site and the facilities it offers.

A company-wide survey attached to a memo informing staff of your Internet plans can start to get people involved. Offering everyone the opportunity to volunteer services as content providers or planners might even help you begin to put together an enthusiastic team to work on the development in an official capacity. Getting as much input as possible will also help stimulate the development of ideas for the new site.

It is vital that employees are informed about how the Internet can benefit them in their working roles. This may be just packaged as what benefits the long-term growth of the company will also benefit them directly. You might offer Internet training days or workshops, encouraging staff to get to know and use the technology. These kinds of project are discussed in greater detail in Chapters 3 and 4 as ways of introducing Intranets and Extranets to staff.

Peters: Getting everyone involved

www.petersplc.com

Peters, the world's largest distributor of Fairline powerboats, produced an Internet site designed to provide information, contact details and a bulletin board for members of the Peters' Fairline Owners Club. To encourage all employees to contribute to the site and provide users with a handy contact list of individuals within the organization, all staff details were listed online alongside photographs of each person. This provided a good talking point and the majority of employees enjoyed seeing their faces on the Internet. The photographs and personal details were laid out in 'business cards' and made a particularly attractive and personable page within quite a technical site.

Segment and target your online market

When you have an idea of how many of your current clients are using the Internet regularly, you can begin to build a picture of what consumers/businesses are available online for you to target. This is an important exercise because it will start you thinking about the individuals your web site needs to focus on. For example, is your major client base 40+ year olds? Or do you want to appeal to sports-enthusiast teenagers?

In the majority of situations, however, knowing how to target a group of people is not so clear. For example, it was important for 24seven (opposite) to define their users according to sex and age, but for a manufacturing firm it might be more revealing to differentiate between the job titles of those online. If you know that decision-makers that have the status and authority to buy your product are regularly using the Web, you can target these individuals and provide online features and incentives that will appeal specifically to them.

Without going into a detailed analysis of the vast number of potential 'types' using the Internet, users can be divided into two major groups: 'seekers' and 'browsers'. Seekers use the Internet to search out particular items of information. They will not spend time exploring a variety of new sites but will use search engines and known research sites to find precisely the piece of information they require as quickly as possible. They are likely to be more impatient, and will not be content to wait whilst heavy graphics download, many even turning off the graphics on their Internet browsers to speed up their time online. These individuals are data driven and primarily aim to access the information that the technology contains.

Browsers, however, spend their time exploring the Internet without such a clear idea of what they want to find. They may initially venture online to access a particular fact or to have a look at a specific site, but they will soon allow themselves to drift to new sites following links or working through a variety of results to searches. These people are more likely to be relaxed and patient online, and will wait whilst graphics and slow technology downloads so that they can view the full glory of each site. These individuals are likely to look more at the abilities of the technology, the animation and 'thrills' a good site can offer, rather than the content or information contained within.

24seven: Target marketing

www.24seven.co.uk

This pioneering UK company developed an innovative shaving and toiletries brand called 24seven. Created for 13–23 year old males, it was designed as a leading-edge, fashionable brand that aimed to coax young men into high street chemists to wear the brand 24seven. Leading up to the launch of the product an Internet site called 24seven was developed to begin the process of brand establishment. This strategy was well formulated: it was known that primary users of the Internet are young males who often have access to computers both at home and at school or university. This was a well-documented audience: their tastes and fashions easily accessed via lifestyle magazines, television programmes and popular music and sports.

A lifestyle site was produced, directed and written by the target audience for the target audience. Rather than being commercial, the site provided newsgroups (including an 'Argue' group), 360° viewing of pubs, gig guides, music/film reviews, and 'cool' links. It generated over 5000 visitors a day.

Within six months a virtual community was in place ready for the launch of the 24seven product. The products themselves were included in the web site as inconspicuously as possible, avoiding any kind of blatant sell.

Your site needs to appeal to both seekers and browsers. It must look interesting and inviting enough for a casual browser to stop and investigate it further, and also promote itself successfully so that a seeker searching for a site like yours can find it quickly in the search engines or through relevant newsgroups, etc.

It is important that you carefully target your web site at a specific desired audience who will be interested in your products and services. It is also important that you consider carefully who will be online, and how their behaviour when using the Internet might affect how they experience your site and the influence it might have on them.

There is a distinct choice that you can make between targeted and blanket promotion both on and offline. Which you opt for will depend partly on the context you have selected for the site. For example, if you produce a site that focuses exclusively on the technical methods used in the production of fibres, it is unlikely that many members of the general public will be interested. Instead, you might stress that their favourite piece of underwear is so comfortable thanks to this fibre. Therefore, which features you pinpoint in your promotional literature and the keywords you use to highlight the site online will determine the kind of visitor you attract.

Who is on the team?

At this stage it is crucial that an internal team is appointed to oversee the project. It would be their responsibility to achieve the

Stages	Skills needed for Internet development
Presentation	Market awareness: whom are you aiming for? Design ability: to convey your company image and message via the Internet. Programming to make your site work. Copywriting: to create snappy, effective content. PR: to promote the site and its launch successfully.
Interaction	Programming: to develop more complex online features like newsgroups etc. Management: to ensure that the site is updated regularly and consistently, and to manage forums etc. Sales: to ensure that the sales process is adequately and successfully represented online. Customer care: to provide quick response to requests from the web site. Marketing: to publicize the competitions and other online features.
Representation	Management: to successfully integrate the new ordering system with existing processes. Operations: to ensure that the distribution infrastructure runs smoothly. Marketing: to make sure customers are encouraged to use the online ordering facility, and know all about it. Customer care: to provide back up and respond to web inquiries.

Figure 3.11   Skills required at each stage of development

objectives set out by your vision statement. By involving members of staff at this early stage, each individual becomes committed to the success of the project. A shared vision can be generated through open discussions. Ultimately, even if an external agency is brought in, there will be a few communication difficulties in designing a project that will correspond with your stated ambitions.

Developing a small, close-knit core team encourages enthusiasm and real ambassadors of the project are created. Keeping the numbers involved to a minimum will generate a focused communication network and force key members to involve other people as well as the team: it should be your ideal that team members cannot stop themselves talking about the new project outside the team.

Other decisions that can be taken at this point include how often the internal team will meet, who will take responsibility for different areas of the project (content, graphics, monitoring success, etc.), and who will act as team leader and assume overall control. Defining the different skills required by each stage will help target the right person for each area of responsibility (Figure 3.11).

As Figure 3.11 makes clear, the skills needed by each stage of Internet development are diverse. To make each stage work first time, it is vital that a multidisciplined steering team is organized to cover all areas of the project. The team should also remain primarily the same throughout each stage of the Internet development. Maintaining continuity will ensure that new input of people and ideas does not result in the site losing impetus. There is always a danger that new people will feel under pressure to make their mark on the project, which might endanger the long-term goals.

The key consideration is for many people to be involved throughout to provide ideas and expertise. However, this can be achieved on a consultative basis, allowing a committed core team to captain the development process itself. It is no good producing the most technically advanced and well-written web site if it is not successfully publicized and promoted.

Whose ultimate responsibility should the Internet be?

IT will often claim ownership; the Internet is on a computer, requires technical skills and will need integrating with the internal systems they manage. Marketing will argue that the web site is an important way to communicate with existing and potential clients

	Skills needed for Internet development
Presentation	Marketing/sales leading, IT supporting
Interaction	Marketing, sales and IT together
Representation	Operations/distribution leading, All departments represented

Figure 3.12   Responsibilities overview for Internet development

and should therefore be part of the overall marketing mix they handle. Sales may suggest that their input is important because the site is being produced to meet the customer's needs, and they have most contact with the customer. Operations and Distribution will also want to be involved if the site is to influence the normal procedures of how goods are dispatched or orders taken.

The only answer is that all departments and disciplines should be involved, or at least consulted, as the project gets underway. The final decision for who should be responsible your Internet project will depend largely on the culture and needs of your organization, and the stage you are aiming for. However, a multidisciplined team will provide a strong foundation of knowledge and expertise that can underpin all decisions. Internet sites are complicated developments that require high level input from disciplines as diverse as marketing, sales, IT and operations, as summarized in Figure 3.12.

Involving an external supplier

If your organization decides to use an external supplier, the same decisions need to be made to ensure that you select a company who can offer all the necessary skills, share your long-term vision and work successfully alongside a central steering group within your organization. An external company needs to be another champion for your project. They need to add lots of new ideas, and have the expertise to evaluate your vision and then work to make it a practicable reality. You need to have confidence in their

24seven: Using an external supplier

www.24seven.co.uk

24seven, a brand we looked at in some detail earlier, used an external supplier to provide a unique service to its target market or 13–23 year old males. A 22 year old man was employed within an Internet marketing company to manage the 24seven web site, updating it every day and responding to comments posted in the newsgroups. This was a big financial commitment, but ensured that 24seven users got to know a brand that went to great efforts to keep them entertained online. Market research showed that each user thought that there was a 'personality' behind the site, that they were talking and listening to some one like themselves who was interested in the same things they were and crucially, was interested in them.

abilities and be impressed by the work they have done for other organizations.

Above all, the strength of your relationship will determine how successful any partnership with an external company can be. Spend time early on introducing everyone to the members of your external team, ensure that communication channels are open before any work gets underway and make certain that your supplier really understands what it is your company is trying to achieve, and why.

24seven was a success because a close and flexible relationship was developed between teams in each company that quickly became a working friendship. In this case an extremely strong relationship grew between a primary content provider in each organization. Each party developed a strong vision of the site and what they wanted to achieve with it, but also had the benefit of multidisciplined teams in each company to back them up with extra ideas and input.

How will you ensure team commitment?

The development of the team as a group dedicated to the success of your Internet project is one of the key determinants of long-term success. Like any printed brochure or promotional document, an Internet site requires a great deal of initiative and attention to detail to get it right. The quality and enthusiasm of the people on the team will be a major factor in determining whether your company achieves its objectives and can then keep the momentum going to ensure that your site is always dynamic and fresh.

Early involvement is crucial, as is encouraging team members to talk about the project and begin to generate company-wide interest and support. Below are some initial questions to ask teams beginning to work with a vision of new technology for your organization.

1 **Where do I fit into this vision?**
   - By describing the overall vision as it affects each individual, each member should begin to identify with the whole.
   - By establishing how the project and goals will benefit each team member further commitment to the long-term success and development will be generated.
   - Each individual will accept ownership of their part of the project, but should be encouraged to recognize the collective responsibility that will be the driving force.
2 **What problems might we face?** An open discussion that focuses on the potential drawbacks and pitfalls each department can anticipate will strengthen the project plan. It will also develop involvement and get everyone thinking about the Internet and its implications.

Stages	Success criteria
Presentation	Increase in total number of clients Market research to establish changing attitudes to your organization
Interaction	Number of qualified leads achieved Time 'live': number of leads resulting in an order Cost of project: resulting revenue generated
Representation	Number of orders generated Cost of project: total revenue generated Revenue generated online: total turnover

Figure 3.13   Success criteria of project

3 **What help may we need?** An open discussion will identify internal weaknesses (e.g. the need for specialist Internet designers/copywriters/programmers) and begin a collective decision-making process to decide who should be involved and at what stage.
4 **How will we best function as a team?** Regular update meetings will strengthen group cooperation, encourage consistent communication and develop the team as a unit that is moving towards one common destination.

How will you monitor, measure and manage your success?

The core team should determine precisely how success would be monitored so that realistic expectations can be defined before the site goes live on the Internet. Your organization needs to define how you will ascertain that your goals are being met and how your long-term strategy might then be influenced by this. This process can be mapped out within the Cyberstrategy Model, as in Figure 3.13. How each organization chooses to measure its Internet success will vary from company to company, but Figure 3.13 details some of the issues that might affect how your site performs, or appears to perform.

Alternative markers

Vouchers can be included within your site that users can print out and take to one of your outlets to receive a discount or special offer. This approach will give you a concrete means of testing how many people are visiting your company as a direct result of seeing your web site. An exclusive online incentive can also provide the ideal focus for an advertising campaign for the site.

Companies have also used a password system that allows users who have accessed their site to quote a secret keyword that entitles them to some form of discount. Travelodge use a system like this as part of their online booking facility. If users visit the Special Deals area of the site they can acquire a secret number that gives them a discounted price when it is typed into the online booking form. For Travelodge this helps to demonstrate how many users are exploring the most frequently amended area of the site and how many are heading straight for the booking section. This provides invaluable information about people's expectations and aims when they enter the site and plays a significant role in decisions about future web developments and what areas of the site to focus on in promotional activities.

Hit rates: A word of warning

Particularly with Stage 1 of the model, when your organization presents itself online, it is important to view your web site as just one component in your marketing mix. It is another tool in the long-term building of your brand and must function in cooperation with the other promotional elements of your marketing activities. To a certain extent, it could be viewed as your flag staked in the future of new technology (Figure 3.14). But quantifying how many people have seen your site if there is no integral feedback mechanism (response forms, competitions to enter, etc.) will be extremely difficult.

Web sites produce statistics that tell you how many 'hits', or visitors the site has received. Modern statistics can also tell you how many users went to each page of the site, what time of day they entered and where they came from. However, these figures are extremely unreliable and do not offer an accurate picture of the success of your Internet site.

Most Internet providers now use computers called 'proxy servers' to help improve the speed of service they can offer their customers. These servers sit between the individual user and the server on which each site is hosted. When someone downloads a page from a particular site, the proxy server stores a copy of the pages. Then, when the next user selects the same site, the proxy server holds a copy of the current version, and will show this to the user. The consequence of this is that users are seeing copies of pages and therefore the servers hosting those sites do not count a hit every time someone looks at their pages. This means that hit rates provided by hosting servers are reading well below the true figure. If you think of the millions of people using an Internet provider like AOL who may all be accessing the same copy of a popular site, the true number of users is likely to be massive.

Therefore, it would be unwise to define the quality of your Internet development simply by the number of hits it appears to get. A much better marker would be the number of enquiries you receive from the Internet, via email or from response forms on the site. These should give you some indication of how much business the site is generating. It is, however, also important to keep questioning your clients when they visit you to do business. Ask them if

Figure 3.14 Staking your claim in new technology

they have seen the site, what they think of it, if it prompted them to get in touch, and so on.

Taking these two information sources together you will be able to build a picture of how successful your site is in terms of bringing business to you. This is particularly the case if you move to the representation stage and offer an online order facility. A company that receives definite orders from their web site will be able to tell you precisely when the development had paid for itself.

What will be acceptable?

It is important that expectations are stabilized and 'set' before the project goes live. The success of the site must be determined in such a way that everyone involved is measuring it using the same quality yardstick (an example is given in Figure 3.15). This will ensure that if the site fails, your organization can respond quickly and effectively to put initial problems right. Over-optimistic expectations will be disappointed, especially because it will take a number of weeks, if not months, for your site to be listed with all the search engines and for even people who know your company well to recognize that your Internet presence exists.

A good way of defining how your site is faring online is to set a number of deadlines by which the project must 'prove' itself. For example, conducting a review of the site and the consequences it has had for your business after 6, 12 and 18 months will develop a true picture of the implications the Internet has had for your organiza-

Stages	Acceptable success?
Presentation	We have a web site we are proud of, and are beginning to implement and learn about new technology. Some new customers who have seen our web site have become interested in our company as a result. The web site has increased awareness of our brand. We have associated our company with new media.
Interaction	As above, plus: We have received some enquiries even if they haven't all become orders – at least people are approaching our company. We have had enquiries from people who might not have considered our company before. We have increased our brand awareness and improved the status of our organization through improved customer service, a new dialogue with clients, etc. Some enquiries have become orders.
Representation	As above, plus: We have received some orders from the web site.

Figure 3.15   An example of setting your level of acceptable success

Stage	Measurement factors
Presentation	Hit rates, considered as under-estimates. Research new and current customers regarding company image, awareness of the site, etc. This will assess the impact the site is having. New enquiries.
Interaction	Hit rates Email and response form enquiries Research, as above Other enquiries Competition entries Vouchers received/special offers
Representations	Hit rates Email Research, all as above Actual orders from the site

Figure 3.16   Measures of success

tion and will aid you in formulating a plan for the next stage. This should take account of the different factors depending on what stage of the model you are working at (Figure 3.16).

How to react when things don't go well

It is also important to have contingency plans prepared for the times when the site does not meet the realistic expectations you have set or that you can implement when you want to increase the market penetration your site has achieved after a period of time. Figure 3.17 outlines some initial ways of improving the performance of your site.

These are only suggestions: it is vital that the steering team within

Stages	Strategies for improvement
Presentation	Publicize the site address: in traditional marketing materials, brochures, on business cards, posters. Introduce Internet specific give-aways (pens, postcards, etc.) that advertise the web site. Tell Internet publications about your site and request reviews: press releases. Encourage your employees to look at the site and tell their customers and acquaintances. Email-shot and mail-shot clients. Post URL in relevant online newsgroups and special interest group pages. (Read their charters to ensure that they will be amenable to commercial entries.) Submit the site to 'cool sites of the day' pages. Check out your search engine positioning and amend if necessary (see Search Engines section of this chapter). Have the site running at every exhibition you attend and in your company reception area.
Interaction	As above, plus: Provide an incentive for the user to respond (free prize draws, competitions, etc.) If the quality of the feedback from the site is poor, ask specific questions on response forms.
Representation	As above, plus: Provide incentives to order online rather than through traditional methods (discounts, free postage and packing, etc.).

Figure 3.17 Strategies for improvements

your organization has 'emergency' action plans and as many ideas as possible for publicizing and developing awareness of your web site and the features it offers.

Planning your structure

It is important to know in some detail what you would like your site to contain, what technology you will need to generate the different features you want and to have a strong idea of how you would like the site to look online. By identifying your business aims and talking to your target market you will have already begun this process. Before any production gets under way it is important to assess and determine the following: precisely what structure your web site will have; what content needs to be generated; what the design should do and how it should complement your current corporate image.

Your research may have provided some indication of a feature that a number of interviewees expressed an interest in. This kind of 'quick win' can be invaluable when the site initially goes live and will provide an ideal focus for launch advertising and direct mailing. For a high tech manufacturing firm this might be a 3D rotating model of their product that interested users can zoom in on and explore in detail. For a restaurant a quick win might mean a fun game aimed at children or an illustrated copy of the menu. For a retailer it is likely to be online offers and full product information. By pinning down precisely what your target market will appreciate can give you some confidence in your site and what it can achieve in the first few months.

In Figure 3.18 we outline the various online features that correspond with some of the different business benefits that can be achieved through Internet development. This provides an extension of Figure 2.3 and is a useful exercise to complete before you make any final decisions about what features your site will contain. If you always approach each element of the content from the perspective of what you want to achieve through it, you can ensure that you are investing your time and money strategically.

These examples should help your organization formulate a structure for an Internet presence that will successfully deliver all the results you have identified.

Even at a strategic level, planning the structure of your site is

Stages	What do you want to achieve?	Online features
Presentation	• Educate clients about your company, identity, long-standing credibility, etc. • Establish financial stability, acquire investors. • Educate clients and potential clients about your products and services. • Allow users to browse at leisure. • Have online resource you can refer enquiries to. • Provide useful and accessible information source. • Information channel for news and fast updates. • Opportunity to provide special offers to potential clients. • Draw new clients into your stores, or encourage past customers to return.	• Company history and mission statement. • About us. • Annual report and accounts. • Catalogue/brochure with full product information. • Frequently Asked Questions. • Briefings/newsletters. • New product updates. • Specific offers and discounts. • Maps of outlet locations.
Interaction	• Gain information about client needs and desires. • Provide fast response to cover problems and give improved customer service. • Discover what clients think about your company and services. • Provide facility for clients to access support and help fast and easily. • Ability to test market new product/service developments and gauge market opinion. • Offer customers a right to reply and influence decisions and developments.	• Easy response mechanism. • Decision tree taking client to most appropriate product or service. • Newsgroups/online conferences. • Automatic responders. • Online customer support. • Complaint handling response abilities. • Market research/test marketing. • Voting mechanisms.
Representation	• Provide fast and 24-hour ordering service. • Offer constant and easy to use online quotation service. • Funnel users seamlessly into integrated ordering system. • Rationalization of internal systems and procedures. • Provide offline access to information.	• Secure online ordering and quotation system. • Online ordering system directed into existing procedure • Hybrid CD-ROM applications

Figure 3.18 Specific examples and benefits of corporate Internet development

essential because it sets the scope of the project and enables you to see the full organizational implications of the development. We would suggest that a diagram be prepared by the core team to provide a working model or map of the site and help to break the different tasks each area will require into manageable components. If you are aiming to develop a presentation site, a basic structure is shown in Figure 3.19.

This site contains a simple layout that offers the user three options to progress from the home page: to find out more about your company, to access information about your products and services and to reach news and frequently asked questions in a What's New section. What's New areas are usually the first places people visit on web sites, and 'frequently asked questions' (FAQs) are also extremely popular as a quick way of getting to know a company and finding out how other people are using them.

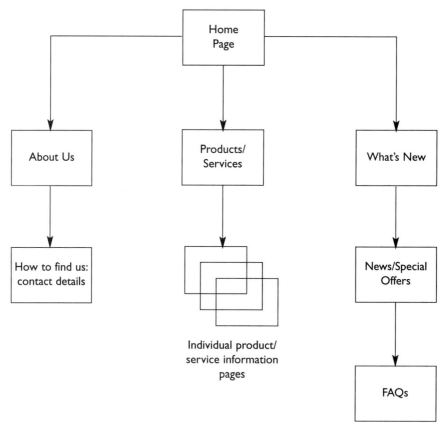

Figure 3.19   Basis Internet site structure

For an interactive site, the diagram might look something like the one detailed in Figure 3.20.

An online forum option has been added to the home page, encouraging users to access this to read what other people have written and then post any questions or suggestions themselves. It is often a good idea to detail on the home page when the forum was last amended so that repeat visitors can see immediately if there is something new to look at. Placing a date on the home page can also encourage users to visit a What's New area that has been recently updated and provides a good first port of call for repeat visitors to the site.

Email facilities are provided in this site. You might want to set up a number of contacts that can receive specific mails. Response forms are a good way of eliciting the information that you want (i.e. contact details, individual interests and needs, etc.). In this site, each area has a response form asking for particular information that is pertinent to that section. In the What's New section, users might be invited to tell their own story, or submit a question or suggestion for the FAQ page.

A competition is also included in this site and given a separate page within the What's New section. The new features need to be the central focus of the site so that users recognize that they have reached a high-level site which offers real added value and interactive facilities. The interactivity will act as the central 'hook' to catch the user and lead them into your site.

Finally, Figure 3.21 is a site diagram for a site that would fit the representation area of the model.

The main addition to this site is the secure online ordering facility which should also be the primary focus of advertising when such a site is promoted both on- and offline. Making the order system as accessible as possible throughout the site is important to ensure that numerous paths lead to it and users always have the option to quickly and easily make a purchase. Most sites achieve this by having a permanent navigation bar on every page that allows users to plot an individual way through a site without having to progress through numerous pages to reach particular areas.

For the purpose of this book, each structure diagram builds on the one before, just as you could extend or reduce your site in the future to move into a different stage of Internet development.

Once the basic structure is in place, responsibility for different areas can be assigned to appropriate individuals within the team.

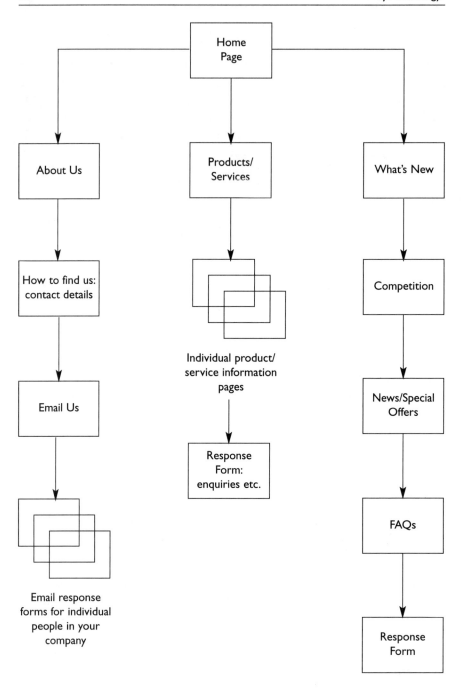

Figure 3.20 Interactive Internet site structure

This diagram builds on the assessment of skills needed begun in Figure 3.12 to define which disciplines will best match each area of the site.

As is clear from Figure 3.22, it is important that numerous people

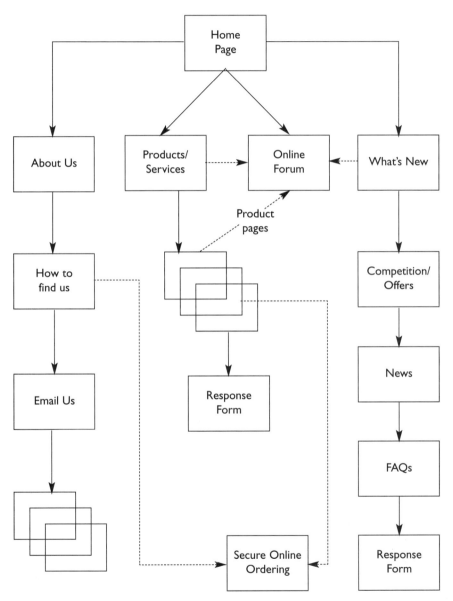

Figure 3.21 Representation site structure

Stage	Area of web site	Skills required (other than technical web skills)
Presentation	Home page About us Products/services What's new: News and FAQs	Marketing and Design Marketing and Personnel Sales, Marketing, Product Management Marketing, Customer Service, PR
Interaction	Response forms: enquiries, complaints, stories, queries, online forum Competition	Customer Service, PR, Sales PR, Customer Service, Sales, Product Management, Marketing PR, Marketing
Representation	Secure online ordering	Sales, Distribution and Operations, Customer Service, Product Management, Marketing, PR

Figure 3.22 Elements matched against skill sets

are consulted about each area. The home page needs to be attractive and striking to entice a user inside your site, but it must also convey the right message and image of your organization. Similarly the online forum will need input from numerous people at different times depending on the kind of attention it generates. Throughout the development of the site, you will also need technical input from the web developers who will create the pages, designs and technical features you need.

Figure 3.23 should begin to give an idea of which areas of the site will require long-term financial and employee commitment. The budget required will increase as you move through the stages of the model, with high level applications demanding more programming, upkeep and support. A high level of involvement will be required at both the interaction and representation stages when responses, competitions, offers and newsgroups demand continuous management.

The commitment the project will demand should be an important factor in determining which stage to aim for. A poorly managed web site can be a very public way of failing to provide customer service

Stage	Level of commitment required
Presentation	Low commitment: Need for updates to the site on a regular basis (e.g. monthly). Press releases can provide a good source of content at this stage.
Interaction	Medium to high commitment: Forums must be consistently managed and contributed to. Response forms must be replied to. Competitions and special offers need organizing and managing. Site content must also be maintained.
Representation	High commitment: All orders must be promptly dispatched and confirmed by usual operations area of company. As above, all newsgroups, forums, competitions, etc. must be consistently managed and responded to. Site content must also be regularly maintained.

Figure 3.23 Level of commitment needed

and disappointing client expectations. Without regular maintenance and updates that add value for users, your site will soon become an anti-advertisement for your company and fail to achieve any of the objectives you have identified. Just as you would not put an old advert in a newspaper, you should not leave an out-of-date web site live on the Internet.

Corporate image and design

When the core structure diagram for your web site has been agreed the actual production process can begin with a map for everyone to work to. This will usually begin with the design, generally focusing initially on the home page that must entice users into your site. It is important that the home page makes a strong visual impact. The page must incite the user to click and want to explore further. Your goal should also be to create a web page that provides a good introduction to your organization and what you do. Through this method you will only get a certain number of people moving further into the site, but they are more likely to be individuals who are interested in what you have to offer. Having said that, a strong design should also encourage 'browsers' to examine your site if only to admire the way it looks: this is all good publicity.

The Internet is helping to turn organizations on their head. Even a matter of 10 years ago, mission statements were created by senior directors and pushed down through the organization. Today, companies have less than four seconds online to convey and prove their USP (unique selling proposition) to Internet users. The mission statement and USP are the primary weapons used in the field to promote brand awareness. They are increasingly becoming more dynamic and operational. Indeed in some industries the unique positioning of the product or service is often produced by viewing the competitive positioning of other industry players. A popular product positioning battle was enacted between Microsoft and Lotus in terms of their GroupWare offerings. The debate was intense online with both responding publicly to the others comments and reviews and the product positioning statements and USPs modifying on a daily basis. As customers will be viewing your Internet site alongside those of your competitors, your USP and brand image must be communicated from the outset.

At the same time as being striking and enticing, your home page must sit comfortably with your corporate image: it is important that when your current clients arrive at your site they recognize where they are, and that new customers get to see your image and persona as early as possible so that it is one they will subsequently recognize offline.

The following example suggests some ways in which a big organization could exploit the Internet to provide direct and personal contact with its clients, and potential clients. For ARRIVA the personal service they offered could begin with an email, or a user getting to know the latest news about the company online. This generated a sense of recognition, and therefore of trust in each visitor to the web site, and increased the likelihood of them using the firm in the future. ARRIVA succeeded in developing a well-known new image in less than six months from its launch, with the web site playing an important role in this building of brand awareness.

The design phase will also force you to bear in mind both the constraints and exciting possibilities of web technology. For example, there are only 216 colours available on the Internet and you will have to work with the knowledge that different monitors will make your final design look quite different depending on how each individual sets their font, screen resolution and colour palette. These can be frustrating limitations and cause considerable problems when you are striving to generate a design concept that will achieve your

ARRIVA Plc: Successful web branding

www.arriva.co.uk

This nation-wide organization decided to develop a new web site when the company updated its image, changing its name from Cowie to ARRIVA. The web site was conceived as part of a long-term strategy to replace the well-known Cowie brand with the more modern image of ARRIVA. A new logo was designed and given pride of place on the new site, as well as on the side of city centre buses throughout the UK and in a series of advertisements produced for central locations around the country.

The web site was tasked with generating a dialogue between the company and its clients, allowing them to see a new side of the organization through direct contact: a new image called for a new media approach. This contact was aided by response forms, a regularly updated Press Office area, photographs of key ARRIVA personnel, and full details for the vast number of ARRIVA outlets around the country. Users would even know the name of the manager at their local ARRIVA motor dealership, how many staff were employed, and the times of day the bodyshop was open for business.

It was important the users perceived ARRIVA as an easily approachable company who were both reliable and capable. ARRIVA outlets are seen as local garages, offering a friendly personal service, and it was important that the web site reflected this approachable characteristic of such a large organization.

aims. At the same time web technology offers great possibilities for designers, from animation and audio capabilities to the opportunity of creating a page that can have the same impact on the audience as a piece of film or video.

Navigation also plays an important role in web design. It is crucial that your site offers a simple and easy navigation system that users can easily pilot their way around. Many sites opt to have a series of buttons that take the user to different sections constantly on screen that allow people to access all the major areas of their site at all times. The way in which buttons are displayed on screen can also allow you to foreground particular features. For example a What's New button that displays when the area was last updated or is placed on the screen in a more prominent position than other options will probably receive most attention.

Animation can also offer quite a subtle way of stressing an important piece of information on the page: Travelodge have their Central Reservation phone number slowly flashing on each page of their site. In this case animation has been used for a reason. Human perception is very sensitive to visual changes and rapid movement attracts the attention. The call to action on this site is to make a booking so the only thing that deserves to be animated is the phone number and 'book now' icon. Many web sites animate logos or other secondary items. This often detracts from the key elements of the site.

We would suggest that you commission experienced web designers, who understand both the possibilities and limitations of Internet technology, to create the central design concept for your site. This can then be translated into web pages by dedicated programmers who will generate the individual pages taking the central design as a template.

We would advise that a number of concepts are considered and test marketed with your employees and select clients before a final design is selected. This can be a good opportunity to recontact the people you spoke to during market research, encouraging them to contribute once again to the development of the site. When you have as little as four seconds to impress someone on the Internet, you need to ensure that you get the design right first time.

Web copy

Web copy is often difficult to get right for the same reason web design can be problematic: the length of time you can hold the users' attention for. People do not want to spend long periods of time reading lots of densely packed text on screen. For many users, staring at a VDU can be uncomfortable and small text often gets quite difficult to see clearly after a period of time. Therefore it is important that all copy is as snappy and newsy as possible. Just like a newspaper, paragraphs should not contain more than two or three sentences and should be well spaced out on the page. Graphics, either photographs or illustrations, can provide good breaks in a lengthy page of text and devices like bullet points and diagrams will also help users to assimilate information more easily.

Again, this is a feature of your site that can be test marketed with both employees and clients. Independent critiques will reveal any areas of copy that might be open to misinterpretation or employ unusual or convoluted phraseology that might appear inappropriate on the Internet. As in emails, people tend to use more informal language on the Internet than would be usual in offline business communication. There is a general sense of the Internet as a community in its own right with separate rules and etiquette set apart from everyday life. The best communicators are sites that embrace this informality and use it to their advantage to generate frugal copy that focuses on establishing meaning rather than adhering to form.

Stressing added value

The ideal combination for Internet content is 90 per cent added value to the user and 10 per cent as a sales pitch for your products and services. The user must visit your site voluntarily and will leave it most content and likely to return if they take something of value away with them. This might just be an interesting piece of information, or an easy and cheap way of ordering their next CD purchase, but your aim should be to send each visitor away better off.

Stage	Focus	Added value
Presentation	Information source.	One-stop information resource. The user can browse at leisure, gradually making their mind up and revisiting different items.
Interaction	Forums. Email response facilities. Customer service provision. Special offers. Competitions.	Ease of contact. Fast response time. Discounts and exclusive opportunities to access competitions and special deals
Representation	Online order system.	Ease of ordering. Speed. Online offers. A relaxed way of shopping. 24-hour access.

Figure 3.24   Added value analysis

Figure 3.24 demonstrates how different features can be focused on as adding tangible value to the end user of your web site. This is what you need to stress as you promote your site both on- and offline.

Test marketing

The design, copy and even the way in which different features of your site are positioned online should all be test marketed before you go live. As we have suggested, your site must be instantly acceptable and liked by a broad range of people and you will only have one opportunity to impress.

Invite a select committee of customers and employees to visit a test area at an URL that you keep private on the Internet or send out printed packs showing the screens from the site and kind of content it will feature. Either online, or as a written or telephone questionnaire, ask them specific questions about the prototype site and then listen to their feedback.

1 What is your initial reaction to the web site design? (Excited, unimpressed, enthusiastic, interested, etc.)
2 Would it be easy to navigate around this site and know where you were going?
3 What areas of the site did you like/dislike the most and why?
4 Was there anything you felt was missing from the site?
5 What would make you go back to the site again?

You might like to make it worth their while to visit the test area and respond to your questions by offering a prize draw, or a discount in return for their help.

This exercise is extremely valuable and will help to ensure that your site does succeed first time with maximum impact. It will also offer a good opportunity for the core team who have been creating the site to take a step back and re-evaluate their work so far.

Launching your web site and search engines

Going live with your Internet site, whatever stage of our model you are aiming for, is an extremely exciting moment for everyone involved in the project. However much time you have spent preparing a site, seeing it live on the Internet is still a fabulous vindication of all of your efforts.

Before you go live with the site you must check the legal position if this has not been a key consideration throughout the project. We have specifically included an Appendix dedicated to providing some guidelines, but this is not intended to be in any way a replacement to definitive legal advice. If in doubt at all, please immediately consult your specialist legal adviser(s).

Next, you need to consider publishing your web site address on all your marketing materials. An internal memo should inform your employees of the imminent launch and the news can be spread to clients through newsletters, mailshots, etc. Issuing a press release will help to flag the new site to journals and magazines and jump-start any press coverage or reviews. Courtaulds Fibres Viscose hand out colourful postcards bearing their web address at each exhibition they attend as a reminder of their URL, whilst Gemini Dataloggers took an alternative approach as detailed in the next example.

Gemini Dataloggers: Launch planning

www.geminidataloggers.com

Gemini Dataloggers is a UK firm manufacturing dataloggers for an international market. All products reach the end consumer through a closeknit network of distributors. This network proved to be one of the key promotional vehicles Gemini could use when its first web site was launched.

Hundreds of little sticky 'spiders' were produced that were just the right size to sit on the top of computer monitors. Each bore the new web address and were sent out to all distributors to be given to customers; they were also taken to be handed out at each exhibition Gemini attended. The spiders were positioned as a good memory tool to remind users to look at the site for the datasheets they had requested during the market research phase of the project. Gemini knew that it was providing something its clients wanted, and employed a fun and quirky tool to let them know that they had done exactly what was asked of them.

As a result the web site received a huge number of hits in its early months live and awareness of the site and the company was boosted extremely effectively.

This was a relatively inexpensive project for Gemini Dataloggers, but generated the right level of interest in its customers and distributors and neatly emphasized its commitment to customer service. Gemini knew its target market well enough to recognize that they would respond well to a quirky character that could be fixed to their computers and remind them of the new site.

Online promotion

However well your site is advertised offline through your marketing materials and the press, it must also be promoted online. This is primarily achieved through keywords or 'metatags' that are placed in the html code of each page and the entry of your site in the various search engines available on the web.

The keywords should be a list of 100 terms that users are likely to use when they search for a company like yours. It is probably worth looking at your online competitors to see how they use metatags and what terms they have selected. You can also test how effective their choice has been by visiting some search engines and typing in some of their words to see where they are listed in the results.

Search engines: The problems and the implications

Just as the Internet is lacking an effective means of monitoring usage in terms of user statistics, it is also an increasingly unwieldy and problematic medium in which to promote yourself. Both are drawbacks for organizations generating an Internet presence, and stems from the sheer size and scope of the world wide web and the lack of regulation that can be exercised over it. In publishing there is some control over what is afforded attention and placed on public display. On the Internet no such mechanism is in place and anyone can, in theory, place whatever information they please live online. This not only makes finding the precise site an individual user is interested in both time consuming and frustrating but also makes the task of the web developer extremely difficult.

Search engines act as evaluators of material presenting the user with a list of sieved and selected pages that are chosen according to the keywords entered. As intermediaries between the user and the mass of information on the web, they are your first port of call when publicizing a new site. When the vast majority of users start with a short list of popular engines (generally, Yahoo! AltaVista, Infoseek, Excite, HotBot or Lycos) whenever they use the

Internet, it is they you must persuade to deliver your pages to an interested audience.

Each engine is a computer that users access to look for new sites. The majority house databases that will either accept submissions from web developers or trawl the Internet to collect data. Each URL is entered in the engine accompanied by a list of keywords and a description (which in the case of Lycos is drawn from the text of the site itself) that the engines use to match with keyword requests from users. In principle this is a relatively simple procedure, but when individual engines contain upwards of 30 million pages, getting your site listed in such a way that the right people will be able to find it can be incredibly difficult. The most popular engines are so busy that it can take weeks, if not months, for each site to appear, if appear it does. It is also possible with the larger search engines for the site to 'vanish' (either deleted or simply lost amongst the millions) from time to time. Each engine imposes rules for entry, but these can be elusive to discover and might alter over time, also affecting your entry.

The search engines used today are far from ideal and make long-term site maintenance and management particularly fraught. It is important that you regularly monitor how your site performs in these databases, changing keywords and re-entering your details as necessary. This can be extremely frustrating and labour intensive and it is a good idea to have someone on your Internet steering/management team who can take responsibility for this role.

Types of engine

- **Robots.** These include a large number of the most popular engines like AltaVista, Infoseek, Excite, HotBot and Lycos. Robots allow URLs to be listed with them and then go out and follow links between pages to generate their database. They will read the whole of a registered site rather than relying on the 100 or so keywords submitted with each web address. This makes robots particularly receptive to long keyword search strings.

  Each robot considers the <title> html tag of a page to be the most important description of the content, so it is vital that you prepare this carefully. The title will appear as a clickable link when your address is listed by the engine, so try to make it read as an inviting description of your site rather than a dull list of keywords. Also, keep it short so that it will be displayed in its entirety.

Results are returned in order of keyword density (i.e. the percentage of keywords within the document), so construct the text of your site carefully with this in mind. Do not waste time with invisible or camouflaged keywords (hidden in the comment tag or hidden in background colours) as some engines will penalize a site for this and not list it at all. Basically, try to include plenty of keywords in the first paragraphs of your site. Some robots will also penalize a site if keywords are repeated within the list, so try to avoid this. Because robots will look at each page of your site, place metatags on every page.

- **Directories (Galaxy, Yellow Pages).** These are lists generated from submitted information only: the onus is firmly on you to spend time inputting all your data. Sites are stored and displayed by category and the engine will not independently look for any additional material about a listing on the Internet. Whatever you enter must do all the work, so spend time constructing an enticing description to appear alongside your site name.

  Because users will tend to search for information by topic, it is crucial that you enter your site in the best place where your target audience will intuitively look for it. This can be a difficult task: if you run a luxury hotel do you list yourself under hotels, accommodation or luxury hotels/accommodation? Try to think as your customers might, and use any market research results that you have. For example, potential Ritz Hotel visitors will probably look specifically for luxury hotels and not wish to search through vast accommodation listings.

- **Categories or free links pages.** No search engine is involved with these pages as sites are input within a category that the user is then free to browse through. Again, the description you enter must be inviting and the location of your listing will be paramount in attracting your target audience. These pages receive lower overall traffic than the other search facilities, but you will be reaching users who are likely to be attracted to your products and services because they are searching within a category that applies to your company.

- **Multiple search engines (Northern Light).** These sites use other search engines to find requested sites for them. When a user makes a request the site sends queries to multiple engines (particularly to the major databases) and then presents an amalgamated version of the top 10–100 of their results. This can make these sites the ideal place to start a general search before a user narrows their target.

- **Usenet newsgroups.** These are areas of the web patronized by regular users who have an interest in a specific subject, activity, etc. Many will accept any entry, allowing you direct access to a target community easily. However, before you start to advertise your site, read the charter for each group to ensure that they will not discriminate against commercial entries. Also, word your entry sensitively to make sure that it is not too overbearing. By going in too strong you may alienate the very audience you wish to attract to your site.

- **Targeted search engines.** These engines are also localized and cater for particular interest groups – regional, trade or industry specific. The same cautionary advice applies as for newsgroups, although there is no need to tone down the sales pitch of your entries in these databases.

Yahoo!

Yahoo! is a particular case that demands its own subheading. Getting a listing in Yahoo! is notoriously difficult and takes considerable time, energy and patience. However, if you succeed, the chances of thousands of people reaching your site are vastly improved, and some research suggests that nearly three-quarters of all online orders arrive at a site via Yahoo!

The engine was set up in the early 1970s and still runs a procedure whereby each entry is verified by a member of Yahoo! staff who know the Internet intimately and are employed to ensure that the database is made up of high quality sites that pass all the necessary tests and regulations. You won't get a listing with Yahoo! unless you understand what they are looking for and do your best to provide it. The fact that humans are judging each and every entry also means that it can take a relatively long period of time for your site to show, even if you make the perfect entry.

To pass the Yahoo! test your site must be a useful and comprehensive piece of quality web design. An amateur one-page advert that takes an age to download is not going to be accepted, but a 10-page interactive guide to your organization will provide a quality addition to the database. Your site should provide some value to the user and look professional and well executed. You must also take care to request a listing in an appropriate category. It is also important that you get your entry right first time as the 'Change URL' form rarely succeeds. Also, do not submit your site before it is complete and fully live on the Internet. 'Under construction' sites will not be listed.

Yahoo! is also likely to reduce the length of your title and your description, so plan these carefully and be as frugal as possible in what you say. Keep the description to one sentence and try to avoid lengthening punctuation or any form of tautology: don't repeat any words or ideas in your title or description, they will only be removed. Make sure that your description is a sentence that makes sense and adequately sums up the contents of the site. Lists of keywords may risk not being listed. You can try to enter subdirectories of your site individually, but the Yahoo! team will probably spot repeated domain names and you risk having your site penalized.

The only sure way of getting your site registered with Yahoo! is by purchasing banner adverts or keywords so that your site comes up on screen when someone searches for something relevant. This is not terribly encouraging, but stresses the need for having someone on your team who can spend the time making sure that you are listed and well publicized by online search facilities: being listed will dramatically improve the number of visits your site receives, so it is worth getting it right.

Before you submit your site into any search engine, take the time to read their hints and tips on achieving a successful entry. Also spend time getting your keywords and the text of your site title and description the best that you can. Select 100 terms that you think your clients might type in when searching for a company like yours. This should not take an age: go for the first words that spring to mind. Having some empathy with your customers is vital for this exercise, as is asking them what kinds of word they think of when they imagine your firm.

In addition, remember that people are more likely to type in the plural of a word (dogs rather than dog) and try to think of as many phrases that they might use as possible. Another reason for choosing plurals is that most engines will find the plural even if the singular is searched for. Similarly, if there is a difficult term that is frequently spelt wrong, include the incorrect spelling in your keywords. It probably worth avoiding common terms: don't include 'and' and other conjuncts and steer clear of Internet terms like 'Internet, web, browser, computer, services'.

Some sites include words that have little to do with their business but they think people are likely to type in. 'Sex' is the most common term used as a keyword, but will not necessarily attract the right kind of person to your site if you specialize in combine harvester repairs.

Finally, test your keywords before you use them. There are software packages available that will predict the listing certain metatags will produce. Alternatively you can visit search engines and type in your words to see what kind of response they receive. Look at what sites you might be competing with and take a look at the keywords of the highest listed sites to see if there are any you could use. However, remember that you need to be as original as possible when constructing your keyword list to beat the others.

Communication opportunity

The development of a web site can provide the ideal opportunity to communicate with your clients and employees about something new and exciting. This can offer your organization the chance to show a fresh side of your company and involve your customers and staff in a fun area of your business. Emails, especially when used in conjunction with a strong web presence, can be a valuable promotional tool. You can send multiple emails to users if you generate a simple database from all the web responses you receive. This is an ideal way to target an audience who already know and have been receptive enough to respond to your site and are likely to return if you tell them about a new or updated feature. Many mail programs will compile a database of email addresses for you and allow you to send one message to multiple recipients.

The most important thing to bear in mind as you go live with your site is that this is not the end: the initial hard work is complete, but in order to keep the site current, up to date and consistently successful the long-term maintenance is just now beginning.

Email options

You can set up a variety of email aliases for each area of your company. These are email addresses that lie over your normal account and can become part of your overall Internet image. For example, the sales department could be called sales@yourcompany.com, and customer service might be given the enquiries@yourcompany.com email address. These are easy to remember and lend a personality to each of your departments, focusing a user's mind on their function and how they can help them.

Large corporations have two options in terms of email organization and establishing a protocol across all departments and, in some cases, countries. Either domain names are set up on a divisional basis, or as derivatives of the 'mother' URL. For example, Chemicals Plc has the central domain name www.chemicals.co.uk, with one domain operating under www.solvents.co.uk. Email addresses within each division reflect these names. The danger with this approach is that if a centralized email system is to be generated in the future, this will be a difficult and costly exercise. Some of the world's largest organizations have been caught out in this way.

Instead, if individual email names are derivatives of the primary name, centralized email can be controlled easily and domain names published that correspond with each department's identity. Therefore, a UK office might be entitled www.uk.companyname.com online.

What next?

The next stage for any organization that has successfully implemented an Internet strategy is what to do next. Just as it is ineffective to have a web site if you do not consistently update it and exploit its full potential, developing the site to incorporate new areas of Internet technology is the best way of using new media to improve your business over time.

Travelodge is a good example of a company which took a measured approach to the development of its web site and the role it fulfilled within the company's overall marketing strategy.

Travelodge, by using some of its existing database capabilities as the backbone of the online database of available lodges, moved through the Cyberstrategy Model in the ways illustrated in Figure 3.25.

The Travelodge web site has developed from a purely presentational tool to become a facility that adds great value to the end user with an online booking system and plenty of interactive features that provide special offers and something tangible for users to take away with them.

	Intranet	Extranet	Intranet
Presentation			
Interaction			
Representation	On-line booking		

Figure 3.25 Travelodge developments

Travelodge

www.travelodge.co.uk

Forte Travelodge developed its first Internet site in 1996. This was a direct transposition of a printed brochure onto the Internet. It looked exactly the same, but offered customers the opportunity to download maps that could expand to pinpoint the exact location of different hotels.

By 1997 the popularity of the web site had increased dramatically and a new development was planned. This new site provided an upgraded version of the brochure, and now incorporated a response mechanism to allow users to email queries straight to Travelodge. This site again proved a great success in terms of hit rates and enquiry generation. The responses from users also encouraged Travelodge to embark on the final stage: representation.

Currently, Travelodge have launched a new-look web site that is only loosely based on their printed materials. The new site has more interactive features, from competitions and 'TalkBack' response forms to exclusive online offers and a regularly updated What's New area. The most exciting part of this new version is, however, the online booking facility that allows users to explore every lodge in the country via drill-down maps, and then make a booking over the Internet. This latest site has seen unprecedented levels of hits and enquiries, and will have paid for itself in online booking after just three months live.

This inimitable success was partly due to the controlled way in which Travelodge gradually incorporated the Internet with its primary booking and promotional facilities. Care was taken to ensure that its clients were online and would welcome this new booking opportunity. The development of Travelodge's executive service aimed specifically at business travellers paralleled the development of the Internet presence. Therefore, there was a business audience who had easy access to the web and a need for a fast and efficient 'desktop' service.

Gemini Dataloggers, as a manufacturing firm, had little option but to develop its web site into an Extranet that could add value for its distributors as well as providing features that would attract the end customers of its products. This firm could not develop an online ordering service without alienating its network of distributors which act as suppliers and ambassadors of Gemini's products.

An Extranet was developed that sat within the online web site, but demanded a username and password for entrance. Each distributor was given the password and then had access to up to the minute product development news and data. Gemini also used this private area as a means for testing new ideas on the people who knew the most about the products and had a vested interest in seeing them succeed. New ideas were floated and distributors offered the opportunity to provide valuable customer feedback and make their own suggestions for the future of the datalogger product. As a direct result of this unique interchange of ideas and knowledge, new products are launched that help to keep Gemini Dataloggers ahead of its competitors and in a market-leading position.

Figure 3.26 maps Gemini's movement across the Cyberstrategy Model.

The Chartered Institute of Marketing took their development further, expanding an initial Internet presentation site to create an Intranet and Extranet to benefit both their employees and clients.

Conclusion

90 per cent of this chapter has been about the planning and 10 per cent has been about implementation. In reality, 10 per cent of the main efforts used to plan will be allocated and 90 per cent of the real organization's efforts will go into implementation. The reason we have put such a great emphasis on the planning is that this is the area where so little attention is given and where most of the disaster recovery work stems. This is based on practical experience of clients who are on their second phase of Internet development and are forced to return to basics to plan again.

We seek to enable you to get it right first time so that you are faster to market and save the costs of redevelopment. This book is about enabling you to leapfrog your competitors and every section of this chapter will ensure you do just this.

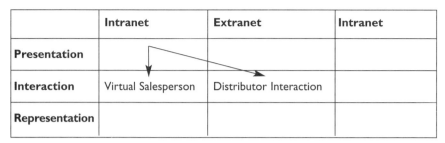

	Intranet	Extranet	Intranet
Presentation			
Interaction	Virtual Salesperson	Distributor Interaction	
Representation			

Figure 3.26 Gemini Dataloggers developments

The Chartered Institute of Marketing

www.cim.co.uk
MarketingNet worked with the CIM to plan out its preferred route of leveraging Internet technology within its business

In 1995, it produced an Internet site internally as a presentation of its organization. In 1997, it came to MarketingNet to move it further into an e-commerce solution. We worked to create an Extranet to communicate more effectively with the branches and have greater control over its Internet site. CIM Direct became its virtual showroom where every item of published information is now available online.

The Extranet was used to create a strong and supportive infrastructure to drive information to the Internet site. News, events and articles were previously centrally controlled and managed and this was not only causing a bottleneck but a huge pull on resources. The system now empowers branches of the CIM to have direct publishing capability.

An Intranet was created to help communicate developments on the Internet and this was called the Surf Board. Diagramatically the movement in the model was as shown in Figure 3.27.

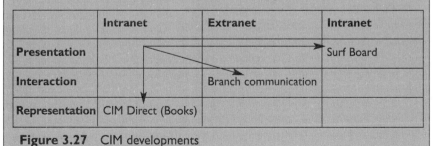

	Intranet	Extranet	Intranet
Presentation			Surf Board
Interaction		Branch communication	
Representation	CIM Direct (Books)		

Figure 3.27 CIM developments

On the Internet

Live on the Internet at: www.marketingnet.com/cyberstrategy/internet we offer you:

- links to organizations we have highlighted and case studies examined in this chapter
- links to other high quality information about this subject available on the Internet
- the ability to discuss your experience of the Internet with the authors and other readers of *Cyberstrategy*
- the ability to post a question to the Cyberstrategy community.

Chapter 4

Your Extranet strategy

Unlike the Internet, an Extranet is not for public broadcast
Unlike an Intranet, it is not just for internal use
Unlike Internet, where Content is King
Now Context is King
Extranets are for targeted meaningful dialogue

Extranets can be defined as commerce-enabled networks using Internet communication protocols to electronically link distributed organizations and/or individuals.

A movement in or an extension out?

They can derive from an Internet site where an area is secured and made private. Alternatively, they can derive from an Intranet where the boundaries extend beyond internal use.

Coming from an Internet site, organizations seek to create a private area where usage is restricted or profiled. It is then either vetted or monitored. The attractions of this route are:

- To protect the information contained by controlling who is allowed access to it. This is especially important for intellectual property which is becoming a key security issue through provision on the Internet
- To encourage and monitor repeat usage through the facility of storing the contact and profiling details
- To encourage ease of future use without enforcing the user to

rekey their contact details. This is enabled through the provision of secure encrypted entry mechanisms (we discuss this later in the section on security)

● To enable a more targeted provision of information in accordance with the preferences, profile and usage patterns of users.

Extending an Intranet, organizations benefit from gaining an existing level of content and active user base which can then be used to provide value to outside stakeholders; be they suppliers, partners, shareholders or clients. The attractions of this route are:

● It opens direct communication channels to closely related organizations.
● It has the potential to add value to every element of the business process.
● It can be developed, prototyped and tested internally first, minimizing any associated risks.

The difference in structure and usage differs depending on the starting point of the Extranet. The term is inadequate beyond a simple technical definition. This chapter provides a framework to enable a business professional to diagnose and conceptualize the benefits and opportunities an Extranet can provide. Only at the end of the chapter do we address the issue as to how best to implement one and outline the most appropriate strategy across the Cyberstrategy Model.

Why are Extranets becoming more popular?

Extranets are commonly referred to as the third wave of Internet evolution. The first wave was Internet, Intranets were second and Extranets are now growing in popularity because they enable targeted meaningful dialogue in a controlled and secured manner.

Most organizational difficulties arise through the distributed communication and management channels that occur within a given business process. Extranets offer the opportunity to streamline and make visible these business processes. In doing so they highlight areas of weakness and enable internal and external market efficiencies to be identified. They allow more precise engineering of who has access to what information, applications and capabilities, mirroring the traditional business cycle and process.

Before Internet technology was deployed in this area, Extranets were extremely costly to implement because they involved building bespoke private networks and customized proprietary programs. These closed system networks made it nearly impossible to build seamless value chains between suppliers and end clients. The main difficulty resided in the lack of a standard common level of networking and communications. The introduction of Internet technology meant a standard protocol for communicating which was inherently flexible, portable, cross platform and forward compatible.

Extranets can provide targeted private communication across organizations. They can be used to mirror any business process that you conduct with any organization. As such they can add value, support or reduce the cost of activities across the value chain. In the next section we use the Porter Value Chain Analysis to help you review how Extranets can add value to your organization.

How critical are Extranets to your organization?

Michael E. Porter asserted that an organization could gain a stronger competitive position (or competitive advantage) by adding value to the end client through its primary and secondary activities. The primary activities are in effect the core operations which define the business process. The secondary functions are the necessary supportive operations which enable the primary activities to take place. This is, of course, a huge over-simplification to what has become one of the most powerful and complex strategic models available in management science today. We are not seeking to define it further than as a conceptual model to diagnose how Extranets can add value across an organization's business process.

The reason we were attracted to Porter's Value Chain Analysis is that it is almost a universally accepted model for diagnosing where

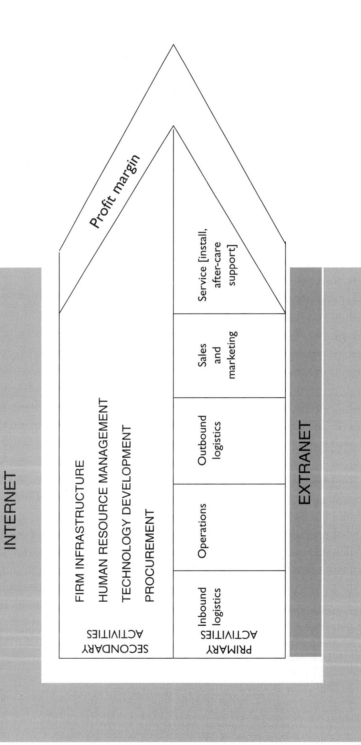

Figure 4.1 Porter's Value Chain Analysis applied to Extranets

an organization can differentiate itself from its competitors. It stems from a fundamental assumption that all organizations seek competitive advantage and that this can only be created in developments or differentiation within the value chain.

Extranets are simply another tool to help an organization improve its business processes in order to achieve competitive advantage. Therefore it is fitting to use such a model to enable a business professional to take an objective and strategic perspective of Extranets.

The value chain analysis applied to Extranet

The first point worth noting is that the driving force behind Intranets is to support the interface between secondary and primary business functions. (This subject is covered in greater detail in the next chapter.) Extranets address primary functions because they provide an outward and inward interface between these business activities and between organizations within which the interaction takes place.

We will now review each of the primary functions in depth.

Inbound logistics–supplier interaction

This can be defined as the business processes used to effectively handle and manage the supply of raw materials or inputs into the business.

One of the key inventions of the 1980s was the invention of just-in-time procurement. This not only improved inbound logistics but in some cases eradicated the need for it by the creation of automatic purchasing controls. The savings and efficiencies obtained were significant and justified the costs of setting up EDI (Electronic Data Interchange) to support the process. Today, organizations can benefit from the advantages of this approach at the fraction of the cost of EDI. Internet technology protocols create a standard platform which suppliers can then standardize as a common protocol of communication to all their customers. In previous times, suppliers may have been forced to comply with several different EDI systems supplied by a number of organizations.

It must be stressed that this ease of supplier communications and EDI is comparative. The exact technical protocols are still in the process of becoming standard. It is important that we do not give the impression that setting up supplier systems is a trivial matter, but it is certainly true to say that it is now considerably easier to achieve than it was in the late 1980s.

The advantage of Extranet for supplier management is not just constrained to online procurement but to the entire supplier communication process.

- Online tendering is possible, where the tender document is held on the Extranet in a restricted area and the invite to tender is posted on newsgroups and sent via email to prospective suppliers.
- Setting up and renewing contracts can be automated.
- Automatic purchase requests can be set up, monitored and adjusted.
- The Extranet can be linked directly with accounts systems and automatic transfers of ease of account query handling.
- Management information about delivery, stock control and cost of production can be provided in real time together with forward projections.
- Online supplier contracting with binding contracts sent electronically.
- One-to-one relationship and account management, where suppliers can gain a greater sense of being in partnership with the organization concerned.

What about service companies?

Porter's model is particularly for manufacturing organizations. For service-based companies, often the inbound logistics handled are people and knowledge. Knowledge management has become a key debate of the late 1990s and the issue of how to reward, motivate and sell knowledge workers is likely to continue into early part of the next century. Copyright and intellectual property management is more critical in today's environment that it has even been. It is not within the scope of this book to open a debate on how knowledge is procured and managed as an inbound logistics task; what we can add to the subject is that Intranets across Europe are being used as knowledge receptacles and much is covered on this subject within Chapter 5.

A hidden benefit is the clean-up and simplification of the supply process

Extranets highlight potential shortfalls or inefficiencies in core business processes such as supply management. Indeed, many of the benefits of Extranet development arise from the fact that, during planning and implementation, the organization is forced to directly challenge and/or mirror business processes. A common reaction to the whole process of implementing an Extranet is in the words of one Operations Director, 'This is what business re-engineering is all about!'

Expanding the supply chain

The opportunity of effective supply management through an Extranet is the potential to widen the boundaries and constraints of traditional supplier management. Internet technology can provide a business case for the use of international suppliers; high technology suppliers who have the ability to deliver higher quality products or reduced costs products through the application of technology, etc.

The level of implementation of Extranets for supplier interaction

Above we have highlighted the extreme use of Extranets for supplier management where the system enables online automatic procurement to be implemented. This is defined as 'Extranet representation' in the Cyberstrategy Model. This may not be possible for an organization to implement and it is common for organizations to start with Presentation and Interaction.

Extranet presentation

Extranet Presentation is appropriate for communicating organizational changes and procedures to new and existing suppliers. It can provide not only a cost saving in traditional communication mechanisms but also a good documentation delivery mechanism which is fast. Examples include:

- contractual information
- procedural manuals
- quality procedures
- corporate structure changes including changes to roles and responsibilities
- contact details of all personnel
- guidelines for supplier delivery
- news items
- new product development planned.

Extranet interaction

Extranet Interaction enables a more meaningful dialogue with suppliers where online response mechanisms can enable an organization to communicate faster, more accurately and consistently. These are ideal if there are a large number of suppliers taking up internal resources. For example:

- A supplier database where the supplier is responsible for updating their own information, e.g. contact details, correspondence information, turnover, employee numbers.
- Tenders or quotations can be created which enable proposed prices to be stored in electronic database format for historical reference.
- Feedback questionnaires on compliance to specific standards.
- Quality control systems which the supplier can link into and request updates from.
- Supplier feedback on attitude and opinion of specific subjects. This is an under-rated opportunity of Extranets where they could be used for a quick and easy mechanism to test market proposed changes or new products.
- Product prototyping when the design of a new product could be demonstrated online and the supplier can be involved in the design process.
- Suppliers actually contribute to the content of the Extranet. Specifically with service suppliers, it is common for Extranets to be the delivery mechanism for actual material, e.g. marketing creative, press releases, articles, scientific papers, business information, multimedia material, training materials, etc.

Operations

The key question here is how Extranets can help an organization to actually produce the product or service of sale. In other words can it be used to actually perform a key business operation?

If an Extranet is to assist in this process it must be the mechanism whereby the actual product is produced online. The actual product or service must exist solely within the Extranet.

A key example of this is online consultancy or advice. It exists only within the interaction online, and will typically be a service delivery where technical support, consultancy or advice is produced online. This could well form a major ingredient to the future nature of consultancy or the selling of intellectual property. A client seeks a solution to a problem and the end product is a piece of information which is created and delivered on the Extranet. Technical support is one of the current major areas – online technical support is delivered in real-time through an Extranet.

The level of implementation

Actually representing a core operation entirely through an Extranet is a select opportunity appropriate only for online service provision. However, within the operational context, presentation of material and interaction can be extremely beneficial. The opportunity to enable the customer to become involved in the production process is immense and adds significant benefit to service-based organizations where the end product is intellectual property or design ownership.

Extranet presentation

If the product or service is bespoke, an organization could benefit from a facility which enables the client to be shown the product during the production process. Examples include:

- Boat building where the client can be presented with the various stages of the boat design and production.
- Design or creative companies can demonstrate alternative designs or early concept work.
- Architects use Extranets to present draft designs to end clients prior to completion.
- Copywriters showing first draft concepts to clients.
- Lawyers showing first draft contracts or legal documents.

Extranet interaction

Indeed, an Extranet could be used further down the line to interactively prototype, develop and produce a product or service. Examples include:

- Interactive prototyping is possible, where the client can feedback online their opinion or choice.
- The client can customize the actual product during the production process, e.g. boat fixtures and fittings, copy production, press release alterations.
- The client can experiment with end touches to the final product using

An innovative PR company

One extremely innovative PR company used an Extranet as the mechanism for clients to get behind the scenes of their company. A client could log on and see a complete archive of all press releases created, the future plan of campaigns, and work in progress. Project plans, and agreed and provisional budgets would be presented. In many ways the clients were given a private viewing of the organization. It was marketed as the unique service offering of this company and it attracted a great deal of interest as a result. Customer loyalty was significantly strengthened and the business processes within the organization have improved remarkably due to the increased openness and visibility from the client's perspective.

prototyping design technology provided by Internet technology. A good example of this type of technology can be found on the Internet within the automotive section where a number of companies have provided the potential car buyer with the option of customizing their car colours (internal and external), finishes, extras and fittings.

A good example of this type of Extranet Interaction was implemented by Caterpillar (as shown opposite).

Outbound logistics and channel management

Before the advent of Internet technology, companies relied on phone, fax and face-to-face mechanisms for logistics of delivery handling. These laborious processes proved extremely cost intensive and drained organizations of resources that could be more effectively deployed in other areas. In many cases the cost of packaging and delivery was greater than the cost of the product, as with:

● software – delivery and installation support were by far the most significant cost of sale
● distribution companies – the cost of communicating the delivery logistics was often more than the marginal cost of delivering the goods
● information providers.

Caterpillar

www.cat.com

Caterpillar Inc opened up its Intranet to an Extranet in the late 1990s. Customers who wanted customized vehicles often wanted to make modifications prior to delivery. These modifications increased the sales cycle time because the process involved managers passing information in the form of paper documents. This correspondence consumed large amounts of management resources.

With its Extranet, Caterpillar's customers retrieved information about their orders and made modifications to specifications online whilst the machine was still on the assembly line. This Extranet reduced cycle time and rework delays and increased customer satisfaction and loyalty. The cost of sale was reduced at the same time as the perceived value of the sales process was increased.

It is not surprising that it was precisely these types of organization which were first to use Internet technology during the 1990s to reduce the cost of outbound logistics. Implemented sensitively it was widely seen as adding value to the process of order delivery because links to internal databases meant a 24-hour world wide service could be supplied.

Extranets in these instances enabled a preservation of the integrity and distinctiveness of the one-to-one relationship whilst reducing the cost, time and effort needed to manage the delivery process. It enabled organizations to upgrade the quality of delivery where human contact was reserved for the purpose of higher level interaction rather than the mundane.

Extranets and Internets are now the standard delivery mechanisms for software. Extranets provide a private download area which includes technical support and the client is emailed a password after authorization of payment. The Internet provides a platform for encrypted software to be freely downloadable where the customer is provided with unencryption information (sometimes for further functionality) post payment and authorization.

Other examples where Extranets are used to handle complete end

Federal Express

www.fedex.com

The most famous implementation of this is Federal Express. This widely written up case study highlights the benefits of Extranets in a Customer Support environment. They effectively replaced a significant proportion of their customer services department by enabling their customers to track the exact location of their parcels/delivery online. With the simple use of a reference number a client could see exactly where the parcel was at any point in time. The cost of implementation was high because they invested heavily in the integration costs of the back office but the business benefits proved to be $US 1 million in their first year.

The other spin-off from being the first was that they leveraged significant competitive advantage and PR coverage. They also forced their competitors into following suit without enabling them to leverage any of the associated benefits they themselves had achieved by being first. This type of service is now considered to be an expected service from world-class parcel delivery suppliers.

delivery are:

- information sales – market research, reports, articles and even books are delivered in electronic form online
- music sales – the music can be downloaded and stored on computer and written to CD
- insurance – the policy document can actually be delivered in electronic format
- banking – the transfer or transaction takes place online
- foreign exchange
- investment management and share dealings
- translation services
- copywriting – the copy is delivered into or from an Extranet
- graphics and design – the artwork is delivered online
- marketing material – the end printer-ready material is sent for approval through an Extranet.

Channel management – managing and supporting agents

For those organizations selling through agents and distributors, filtering information direct to the end client can be frustrating and difficult. Communication cascade can often be inconsistent or slow through traditional channels (e.g. print, telephone, fax, face-to-face, etc.). Extranets provide not only the ability to communicate more centrally but in a more focused way to distributors. The same environment can also be supplied to the end customer as a way of adding value to the distributors.

In the Internet section, we describe how manufacturers often develop Internet Interaction because they can add value to their marketplace by having strong and meaningful dialogue with the end customer. If handled sensitively, this adds value to agents and distributors because it reduces the amount of product support required from them.

In this way, Extranets are unique in that they enable you to manage, control and communicate with your distribution channel. It supports the process from distributor recruitment all the way through to managing the end customer relationship in a cost-effective way.

Channel management – the attraction of trading direct

In the past, it has been costly to set up distribution chains and expensive to experiment with going direct to the next tier down in the distribution chain. With the immediacy of Internet technology, the ability to bypass elements of the chain and achieve higher margins has never been greater. This further supports why Extranets have become extremely attractive.

The interesting development of Internet technology is that it provides a route for organizations to experiment with jumping down a level in the channel with fewer financial risks. Manufacturers often provide a support environment through an Extranet to enable end customers to gain information direct from the source of the product. This enables them to provide a good dialogue with the end customers. They can often then find themselves in the position of being approached to sell direct when the margins look tempting and they have already built up some retail experience.

In this way, Extranets are significantly impacting large distribution chains because they encourage suppliers, distributors, wholesalers and retailers to contact each other directly. Agents and organizations in the middle part of the supply chain are becoming increasingly nervous and we are currently seeing many pre-emptive strikes to ensure a foothold is achieved and not eroded.

A word of warning

80 per cent of manufacturers have been disappointed with the Internet as a mechanism to go direct to the end client. Their failings are not to do with the technology but mainly stem from:

- the lack of the necessary marketing and retail expertise
- the lack of resources to back and implement both the campaign and the necessary supportive internal distribution capability
- the resulting backlash from distributors who then refuse to supply their products
- the negative effects of bad PR.

Sales and marketing

If the Internet is compared to an advertising medium, Extranets can be compared to targeted direct mail. Organizations use them to profile and segment their customer base and privately direct visitors into more commercially confidential information. This generates a more intimate sales dialogue and increased customer loyalty.

The most immediate benefits of Extranets for the sales and marketing function is accountability, confidentiality, the ability to build a one-to-one relationship and customer communities. This circumvents the major pitfalls of the Internet which not only prevents you from detecting who is viewing the information but also risks exposing your business processes to potential competitors. We explore each of these in turn.

Accountability

Extranets are private and only permitted users are allowed to enter the secured entrance. In some cases, this security is not to protect the information but more to profile the user pre-entry in order to direct the client to pertinent information and monitor what they do inside the Extranet. This accountability is extremely important for both customer and product feedback.

By forcing users of the Extranet to register and profile themselves, you are setting up an in-built control mechanism. This coupled with a monitoring system logging where the user goes in the Extranet means that you are building an intelligent customer profiling system. This can not only be used to recognize particular customer needs but also to accumulate product interest over the whole customer base.

This characteristic of Extranets has been especially leveraged by organizations who are restricted in their ability to trade or promote themselves globally. By demanding a registration process and a disclaimer informing the visitor of geographical restrictions in viewing the data, the organization can prove that the information is being restricted to their local market.

It must be stressed that users of the Internet are averse to filling in online registration forms and restricting sales information only within the Extranet is not advisable. However, promoting the benefits and in-built value of the Extranet from within the Internet site will enable you to attract serious clients to take the necessary next step. If it is clearly explained that profiling and registration will provide the end client with a more meaningful dialogue, this can often counter-balance user aversion to an online form.

A vital ingredient to online registration is the ease in which it is executed. If the form is easy to fill out and the process by which the password is supplied is fast, then Extranets effectively enable you to qualify customers through an online filtering process.

Instant online registration is desirable but inappropriate if the Extranet contains commercially confidential information. In this instance, security must be reviewed carefully; we cover this aspect later in this chapter.

Confidentiality

For organizations that capitalize on the knowledge and expertise built into their products and services, Extranets are a preferable channel to market over and above the use of the Internet. It enables a level of confidentiality appropriate for clients to discover the USP without openly differentiating the organization and providing extra information that might aid your competitors.

The level of confidentiality can be graduated to suit the needs of the target audience. For high level clients, you are able to provide a level of openness beyond what is expected and gain considerable kudos from doing so.

Confidentiality agreements can be displayed on initiation to the system and the visitor forced to click an 'Agree' button before progressing through to the Extranet. This is legally binding so long as it can be proved that the end visitor cannot have accessed any of the material without having first accepted the online terms and conditions. In this instance it is imperative that you seek legal advice to ensure that you are adequately covered.

Targeted one-to-one electronic commerce relationships

Knowing who is logging in enables your organization to offer a customized and individual experience that can be dynamically generated and adapted from information about the users' level of security, preferences or usage patterns and a combination of all three.

Again this is especially useful for knowledge-based companies who restrict and reveal their level of intellectual property based on the level of relationship with the client. In this instance, pre-registration must be built in so that strong security channels the client to the correct level of entry into internal databases. The conflict of forcing clients to fill in online registration is by-passed and intellectual property controlled in the most secure manner.

For organizations not providing high levels of intellectual property, Extranets provide unprecedented opportunity to present relevant product and service related information and other valuable content to a targeted, interactive user community through a one-to-one channel.

Once profiled, a database can be kept of each customer: when they visit the site; where they regularly return; what further information they provide; what files they download, etc. The first meaningful dialogue on profiling the customer is logging where their need or interest lies. If the Extranet is segmented, the profiling can enable you to direct the client to the area most suited to their requirements. You can also profile how the user wishes to be provided with information. Some will want to have it on a needs-pull basis and be content to access the Extranet when they have a specific requirement. Others will want an alerting service where updates are sent to them proactively either through automatic faxes or email. It is imperative that this segmentation of information and delivery channels be thought through and tested for acceptability. It is also important that the profiling is not too prescriptive as this will reduce the cross-selling opportunities.

It is essential to involve clients in the development process in order to avoid your Extranet presenting information overload or a negative reaction to unwarranted emails. In addition it is important to set up an easy process for the client to opt out or modify their user profile. Test marketing of the concept, usage and acceptability is imperative and organizations that fail to do this run the significant risk of over-developing a service offering that is neither liked nor required by their customer base!

E-commerce is facilitated easily because the customer is a known entity. It is extremely effective at providing the sales and merchandising channel which simultaneously streamlines the merchant value chain. Again we see here the additional benefits of enabling you to re-engineer the sales side of the business in a controlled and private manner before you open this up to the general public.

Online communities

Interactive communities are emerging on the Internet because information travels faster, is not constrained by time zones, enables large groups to congregate seamlessly and is extremely cost effective.

On the Internet, target audiences are demanding more and more added value. Content is delivered to them at the touch of the button. On Extranets, target audiences are demanding more and more added value. Content is delivered specific to their context. Creating communities solves the huge drain on company resources as you are effectively facilitating your users/members providing content to the rest of the user base.

Community systems vary according to their level of openness. Commercial communities by their very nature need to be closed, especially if the community is sharing specialist knowledge with commercial value. Non-commercial, open communities have the potential to grow exponentially, especially if researched and developed by an existing online community.

Mentors Forum from Hertfordshire TEC

www.mentorsforum.co.uk
Created in 1998, this innovative community system derived in part from an existing Mentors community already established in Hertfordshire. Hertfordshire Training and Enterprise Council (TEC) set up a Mentors Forum as a response from local organizations and individuals who sought an environment which facilitated mentoring relationships within organizations and across organizational boundaries.

They wanted to promote the concept of mentoring across the UK and Europe and demonstrate best practice. They also sought to educate other interested parties about its benefits and the process by which mentoring groups could be established.

Mentors Forum was launched in June 1998 with the sponsorship of the ESF (European Social Fund) and, although 90 per cent of the site is open access to the public, there is an online community using the newsgroup and news bulletin section which requires registration. The project was implemented with close involvement with the mentors' community within Hertfordshire. The concept was also market researched and test marketed with this group.

The design concept for the site was significant, as it needed to be attractive, unique, inviting and fast.

The technology to be deployed needed to be easy and non-technical as the target audience were not significant Internet users. The way that both a newsgroup and a bulletin service were integrated into the site is a demonstration of best practice – seamless from the user perspective.

A significant requirement from the real life community was that it provided a good sign-posting service for visitors from all around the world. The community was keen for the site to be seen as inclusive and as helpful as possible and not to excite the visitor without providing an easy mechanism for them to take the next step. The implementation was a superb network section, which lists mentoring groups and sites across the world.

The results and interest that the community has achieved has been extraordinary and it continues to grow and exchange experiences.

Another example of this is Galileo.

Galileo

www.galileo.co.uk

Galileo, a wholly owned subsidiary of British Airways, is one of the market leaders in computer reservation systems in the world. The main driving force for creating an Internet site was to move quickly into providing an Extranet for its suppliers.

Galileo's clients often needed to integrate their own software and hardware with Galileo's reservations systems. With the huge number of clients and the large range of diverse software offerings used by their customers, Galileo works in close partnership with key third-party software developers. Internet technology has been able to bring immediate benefits by allowing Galileo to communicate quickly and effectively with different system developers.

All the system developers were invited to a conference for a preview of the launch of the Extranet site in 1997. 100 per cent of the target audience were delighted with the offering. It provided fast, effective download of the latest software updates to the existing version and a hot link into the technical support department. What was most interesting was their perception of the discussion area contained within the Extranet. Galileo recognized that, in many instances, these software developers compete for business and had specifically designed the discussion area to be anonymous and closely managed by the technical support team. The system developers were not only happy for their names to be published but keen to actively seek and give advice to other system developers. In this way a community was born which had not existed in reality but facilitated by online technology. It continues to add value to both the third-party developers and Galileo.

Service

After-sales service and support can be provided more cost effectively, more freely available (24-hours, world wide) and more in depth. The advantages for the organization supplying the service are that it is electronic, self-documenting and can be handled in batch mode rather than waiting for telephones to ring. This is commonly based upon a database of information about the product: specifications, manuals, common faults (bugs) and work arounds, etc.

Most of the large software houses use Extranets for technical support. In addition to providing a direct route into the technical support team, it is common for a Frequently Asked Questions (FAQs) section to be included for self-diagnosis. The advantage of this is out-of-hour support with the ability to post actual software modules, updates and bug-fixes online in real-time.

The other major plus point is that it can provide all the benefits of the Internet as a communication channel, but is targeted only at existing customers.

Presentation

Manufacturers of complex technical products provide download-able manuals and specifications to existing clients as an after-sales support service. This also adds significantly to the channel (agents and distributors as discussed above).

Gemini Dataloggers

www.geminidataloggers.com

Gemini Dataloggers is an extremely successful manufacturer of dat-aloggers in the UK. These devices can monitor and capture data pro-files of temperature, humidity, shock, wetness, etc. It has over 40 world-wide distributors.

Gemini Dataloggers was attracted to the Internet as a means of supporting end customers of its products and in doing adding value to the distributors. Their Internet site contained:

- case studies of the use of its products
- a virtual sales person taking the end client through a complex decision tree to help them arrive at the most appropriate product for their needs
- downloadable specifications, manuals and demos of the products and the accompanying data capture software
- information about new products due on the market shortly
- contact information for easy purchase.

The distributors were delighted. The site provided a meaningful dia-logue with the end customer and was a superb communication vehicle that lightened the sales process and administration for the distributors.

But Gemini Dataloggers wanted to go further. It couldn't enter the area of e-commerce because this would damage their distribution channel, which was working superbly. Instead, the company invested heavily in creating an Extranet.

Distributors were each given a unique name and password that enabled them to access the Extranet through a log-on screen held within the Internet site. Once into the Extranet, distributors could download the latest versions of software, read launch plan documents and future product specifications. They were provided with direct contact information with key managers within Gemini Dataloggers and actively encouraged to contribute to the Extranet and Internet sites. This created a virtual community of distributors and significantly improved the communication process. The majority of the distributors continue to use this channel as the main communication mechanism with Gemini Dataloggers. Gemini Dataloggers discovered that whilst the Internet site provided improved customer service, the Extranet increases the effectiveness and cost-efficiency of the communication process.

For service-based companies, Extranets offer the ability to provide after-sales support through an online knowledge-based system. The customer also has the opportunity to correspond electronically with the support team.

Other examples of Extranet benefits include:

- post training course evaluation where the response is held within a database
- news and product updates provided in a dynamic section for customers only
- customer newsletters and upgrades to software products.

Interaction

It is common and often valuable to provide a discussion area or forum where your customers can discuss applications of products and services with other customers as well as with the support team within your organization. The majority of user groups are now being converted to electronic formats. This is mainly because it is the most cost-effective route to achieve wide communication across geographically distributed personnel, providing an easy link to exclusive information and contacts. The perceived value of this for your customers will be extremely high.

	Inbound logistics	Operations	Outbound logistics	Sales and marketing	Service
Presentation stage	• Quality manuals • Policy and procedures • Contracts and terms and conditions • Contact directory • Product news	• Display of customized product or service • Early design demos • Prototyping	• Delivery of visual of end product • View or information about delivery of end product	• Demonstration of expertise • USP positioning • Access to internal databases • Profile determined • Context specific	• Automatic responders • Frequently asked questions • Knowledge databases
Interaction stage	• Online tendering • Product test marketing • Online questionnaire • Self-maintaining supplier database	• Interactive prototyping • Collection of feedback	• Interactive delivery or installation queries • Interactive customer support on delivery	• Order placement • Stock queries • Price queries • Profiled discounting • Targeted email direct marketing • Virtual sales person	• Online customer support • Complaint handling • Market research/ opinion • Voting systems • Newsgroup conference • Email subscription
Representation stage	Online procurement handling: • Collection of electronic material • Automatic purchasing of replete stock • Inventory management	Online operations: • Online consultancy or advice • Online technical support • Electronic banking or dealing	Online delivery of end product: • Software • Music • Insurance • Information • Consultancy • Design, etc.	Online order capture and promotion • Direct continuing dialogue with clients	Complete online customer after sales support

Figure 4.2 Summary of the primary operations of the Porter Value Chain Analysis superimposed with the Cyberstrategy Model for Extranets

Assessing the business case

In the previous section, we have discussed in depth the value of Extranets across the value chain of an organization. The key benefits of an Extranet are:

- to outwardly improve by:
  - Providing new services
  - Improving value chain relationships
  - Increasing competitiveness
  - Increasing customer loyalty
- to inwardly improve by:
  - increasing employee motivation
  - increasing teamwork
  - enhancing communication, service and support
  - facilitate business process re-engineering efforts.

Figure 4.3

We have highlighted how they can be used to improve value chain relationships. Extranets are in effect private Internets or externally rolled out Intranets. They carry with them benefits from both. Most of the internal benefits derive in the whole from the impact of the Intranet as outlined in the next chapter.

Because Extranets simply improve the way you do business, it is practically impossible to perform any useful cost-benefit analysis. Only your organization can judge for itself the value an Extranet brings and at what cost. In order to produce a cost-benefit analysis, we recommend taking these as individual subject headings and applying them to your organization.

Implementation

Because an Extranet either derives from an Intranet or an Internet site, much of the issues of implementation stem from the corresponding chapters. However, there is one main area which needs to be specifically addressed with regard to Extranets and this is security.

Security

The security policy and protection of data

Extranets by their very nature are open to select audiences and closed to others. Therefore there are two main elements to consider: the privacy of the information and the identity of those using the Extranet.

There needs to be strategic consideration of the level of protection of the information. If the information does not contain intellectual property, it is still likely to be commercially sensitive. It contains value and this must be measured and systems put in place to protect it.

The key to this is in referring to the firm's security policy. A security policy outlines an organization's attitude towards what is acceptable commercial risk. It contains the procedures that are considered adequate to implement this chosen level of risk. Just as an organization makes a decision about its level of service or quality, a decision about security is imperative.

This policy will also outline the organization's attitude and policy towards the information, data, backup, virus control and recovery. Typically the security policy will state how and what level of information can be opened to which target groups.

In some cases, security policies may state: 'all information is to be classified as highly confidential and not to be shared with any third parties outside of the context of needing it to conduct business'. If this is the case, an Extranet must only contain information that would be automatically shared with clients and suppliers in the process of doing business with them.

In most cases, the security policy will identify levels of confidentiality pertaining to specific grades of information. This is then graded in accordance with the policy. Highly confidential information will be classified as such and all the traditional mechanisms of protecting this data must be reflected in the Extranet.

Because the security policy will be signed off by the Chairman and may not have been written with Internet technology in mind, negotiation should take place as to how this can be adapted or modified. You will need to consider how it affects any Extranet plans that are in place.

No matter how small the organization, a security policy should be in place. Before any implementation of an Extranet takes place, key decision-makers within your company should decide what information needs to be protected and the level of openness your organization desires, and produce a document to this effect.

Identity and registration

Once this is in place and the implementers of the Extranet are clear as to their organization's policy towards security, consideration must then be given to how the system will identify the users of the system.

Customers may well be given access to pricing information, which is specific to their organization, and the potential for the system to accidentally give them access to other customer or supplier information could be extremely damaging. Your organization must decide how much protection it would like to achieve for the Extranet.

At one extreme, a simple name and password can be supplied on an Internet site to gain entry into the Extranet. This can be shared across all users of the system. This is probably the lowest level of security available and the potential for determined intruders must be considered. If public broadcast of the information contained within the Extranet could significantly damage the organization, this route should be discounted immediately.

To increase the level of security, digital key technology and encryption technology is used. This is included in some applications such as Lotus Domino but can be purchased for the Internet from various suppliers. This combination means that the user of the Extranet is provided with a special identity stored on their computer which the system detects on entry. Only permitted users can therefore unencrypt the information contained within the Extranet. There are many other issues surrounding security and it is not in the scope of the book to cover these; neither would it be feasible to do this subject justice in print because of the speed of innovation in security. Practical sources of advice on security, virus protection and other issues contained in this chapter can be found at:

www.marketingnet.com/cyberstrategy/security

	Internet	Extranet	Intranet
Presentation	A ←	— 1 —	→ D
Interaction	B ←	— 2 —	→ E
Representation	C ←	— 3 —	→ F

Figure 4.4 Matrix for development

What next?

Your Extranet is likely to contain elements that exist at all three levels of the Cyberstrategy Model (see Figure 4.4). At whatever level each of these elements are (1, 2 or 3), you have two directions to pursue. You either:

- **move to Internet (A, B or C).** This involves rolling the Extranet out to the general public or allowing access to a wider target audience.
- **move to Intranet (D, E, F).** Here you create internal systems and procedures to enable employees within your organization to have a seamless interface to the Extranet and the customers or suppliers that use it.

Internet – the next step

The advantages of moving to the Internet are that you are effectively using the Extranet to test market your Internet strategy within a controlled group of existing clients. This significantly reduces the risk your organization takes when publishing information on a world-wide communication system.

Moving from 3 to C has the potential to derive the largest business benefits. Organizations that have moved quickly from F to 3 to C have been the ones to exploit significantly the opportunity of Internet technology. A good example of this is where an organization has linked the retailer's point of sale terminal to a supplier's delivery system where the stock is automatically reordered or delivered direct.

Intranet – the next step

For some organizations, moving to Internet is neither desirable nor appropriate and therefore the key challenge of the organization is to make the interface between the Intranet and Extranet seamless and effective.

Conclusion

The development of Extranets can have dramatic effects on the way that organizations conduct business.

They can support, add value and reduce costs across the whole value chain. They can enable you to gain competitive advantage or obliterate your position in the supply chain. Within the organization, they can improve morale and productivity. They can enhance all aspects of communication. Most of all, they can help you re-engineer the way you conduct business today.

Out of all three implementations of Internet technology, Extranets have the potential to transform how you do business. We have only just begun to grasp how Extranets will transform business as we know it today.

On the Internet

Live on the Internet at www.marketingnet.com/cyberstrategy/extranets we offer you:

- links to organizations we have highlighted and case studies examined in this chapter
- links to other high quality information about this subject available on the Internet
- the ability to discuss your experience of Extranets with the authors and other readers of *Cyberstrategy*
- The ability to post a question to the Cyberstrategy community.

References

Porter, M.E. (1985). *Competitive Advantage: Creating and sustaining superior performance*. The Free Press.

Porter, M.E. (1998). *Competitive Strategy: Techniques for analyzing industries and competitors*. The Free Press

Chapter 5

Your Intranet strategy

> Ultimately technology is not just a question of machines and systems but of power and how power is allocated.
> Karen Nussbaum, *Office Automation: Jekyll or Hyde?*

If Internets are likened to a beautiful cosmetic makeover, Intranets can be likened to the overnight emergent cream, which you apply to bring out the spots. They highlight all the warts your organization has and brings them to the attention of the key decision-makers. They are the most politically sensitive of all applications of Internet technology. They both empower employees and expose them. They have the potential to deliver the most business benefits but in doing so necessarily involve power shifts. This is why planning and objective setting is paramount and the process of involvement critical to the success of an Intranet project.

Power struggles into business plans into action

This chapter highlights the political issues involved within an Intranet. It then goes on to describe the benefits and costs involved in order to provide a structure to an assessment of the business case. Lastly we outline the issues for implementation to enable you to plan a professional, robust Intranet which delivers the business benefits you have planned.

The political minefield

The key political issues confronted by an Intranet are:

- Centralized control, decentralized ownership – the internal battle
- International control – the ego battle
- Departmental competitiveness – the real front-line
- Fear about loss of recognition and influence at all levels of the organization
- Fear about loss of employment at all levels within the organization.

Centralized control, decentralized ownership – the internal battle

For most of the 1980s and 1990s, IT investment was committed to centralizing and integrating information through the use of networks. The IT jargon generated during this period all suggests this business need for centralization and integration. The main terms are:

- Expert systems – created to centralize 'know-how'
- EIS – created to centralize management information
- Document Management – created to centralize administrative data
- Data Warehousing – created to centralize data collection and retrieval
- GroupWare – created to centralize team communications.

All of the above acted as packaging around a concept of a database which pulled information together in such a way that it was easy to retrieve. We do not intend to demean the technical and structural complexity this involved but simply to consider these words in a wider context. Most of the above involved relational database technology combined with effective interfaces. Central to all these was the need to understand data, its functions within an organization and the outputs needed. Effective implementation required a strong understanding of 'people' needs and this is where many of the technologically driven projects failed. Suffice to say that they were all seen to benefit organizations as a means of enabling them to work smarter, more effectively and more efficiently.

Intranets are very much a derivation of this movement. They seek to centralize corporate communication. The main difference is that typically they are less structured. With a centralized sales and marketing database, you know what data is to be captured, how it is to be retrieved and what the interface should look like. With an Intranet, it would be nearly impossible to define what format is expected for each communication. One communication could be a corporate change strategy; another might be an online quality manual. It is much more nebulous.

Internet technology was the ideal solution for many organizations wrestling with how they could communicate powerfully but in a relatively unstructured manner. It offered the combination of graphics and free format text – in effect acting as an internal publishing facility. At one extreme an Intranet might be an organization's internal magazine and therefore be completely unstructured. As senior managers could see, touch and understand information on the Internet, it enabled them to see the power of technology used within their organizations. It released them from the bounds of having to translate their needs into structured formats for interpretation by technologists. Internet technology increased the speed of delivery, which historically had meant that applications were always being built to address yesterday's problems.

On the other side of the fence, IT personnel were the bastions of the corporate entity diagram. This was a diagram of the core data elements which had to be held and managed by the organization, e.g. customer data linked to product data linked to invoicing data. This was the Holy Grail for many companies: a resource where all information was centrally held, managed, controlled and enabled to be presented in different formats for differing customer needs. Power bases arose because senior executives wanted control of organizational data. If this was to be realized, IT teams needed to be tasked with a centralized data clear up: 'structured data'. The fear of the late 1980s and early 1990s was that data was 'getting out of control' and, in order to ensure that it did not, senior managers were happy to bind themselves to strict procedural methods and approaches to ensure centralized data occurred.

IT personnel became honoured and respected for their strong autocratic style of data specification and management. Companies were praised for the effective use of relational technology that resulted in improved customer service and cross selling. Governments with non-interconnecting databases were derided.

Figure 5.1   Business executives sometimes don't know the language to describe their needs

Therefore it comes as no surprise that IT people were insulted and threatened by business demands for cosmetically sexy but clearly unstructured technology such as Internet/Intranet. Most IT departments were either openly hostile or dismissive towards it. They permitted and often helped with the implementation of the Internet. However, when senior managers began to see it as a tool that might loosen internal data harnesses, IT departments saw its potential to undo what had taken 10 years to achieve. Open hostility was usually the result.

In some cases, IT departments were bored of being trapped in structured data management and jumped at the chance of letting their hair down. In these cases, IT personnel saw this technology in the same light as they had the structured data applications. They saw it as their domain and again put up barriers to the entry of average users.

In most cases, Intranet technology also fired the big IT debate: 'centralized or decentralized'. PCs had been the 'wonder-drug' of the 1980s. They empowered users but also cost organizations greatly in cost of ownership. IT departments had to pay the cost of decentralization through increased maintenance demands, backup, support and management. The cost of decentralization was huge and it was soon visible on the bottom-line as organizations struggled with increased PC costs that did not translate easily into business benefits. Large software and hardware suppliers provided tools like client/server technologies that enabled organizations to pull in the reins. Why then were business professionals still seeking to introduce decentralized software control such as Intranets?

Figure 5.2   The benefits of technology explained to the board

The more business executives were attracted to the technology because it freed them from constraints, the tighter the hold the IT departments kept on the reins. Intranets became the hot political potatoes of the late 1990s. The pure simplicity of the technology meant that it threatened power bases. It is no wonder that Intranets are highly political.

The irony of the situation is that IT and business professionals are fundamentally on the same side and that Internet technology is a superb tool to strengthen and support both in their desire for results, recognition and success. It actually provides the mechanism by which business executives and IT departments can communicate faster and more clearly than ever before.

International control – the ego battle

These power battles are strongest when the organization is part of a group. Intranet technology then becomes not only the battleground

An IT department

One innovative IT department used Intranet technology as a way of opening up their department. They implemented an Intranet, which had at its core the development schedule for applications. They presented project plans and publicly presented their time sheets. This gained them instant accolade. Not only were they demonstrating the effective use of this new technology but building a communication about something which was dear to the heart of every department – when applications were to be built and by whom. By opening up their department, the IT staff were in a superb defensive situation to react to business demands for further developments that used the technology. They could react positively by asking what projects should be stopped to accommodate these new demands. They soon found that departments made informed decisions as to which was more important. They acted quickly and placed themselves in the more powerful position.

between IT and business professionals but also between competing IT departments and international departments. The key political issue is nothing to do with the technology but focuses on which team should develop a significant and highly visible corporate success story. The majority of the discussion to determine which department takes control is usually centred on either technical competency or position in the hierarchy, although most players are aware of the hidden battlefield of internal recognition and job security.

Particularly in the case of international companies who have a US subsidiary, there is the greatest potential for conflict. The US were primary movers in the development of the Internet and as such see the technology as an American innovation. The business case as to why any development should therefore be handled in the US is extremely strong.

The underlying issue is concern over who is in charge of internal communication, who is the primary mover and who has the most to gain in being the agent for the implementation. In all cases the head office or holding company takes the first step. Despite often hostile efforts by subsidiaries who would see this as their domain, this usually became the status quo. In some cases, a subsidiary might make the first step which prompts action by the head office, but this is usually short-lived.

Departmental competitiveness – the real front-line

Intranets can provide opportunity for glory as well as neglect, becoming internal billboards that highlight tangible results. Marketing can air their latest brochure at the touch of a button; Quality Assurance can publish dynamic handbooks and quality manuals; every department has something to gain from access to the visible billboard. Key issues here are who gets to go first, who gets access to the glory first and what signals does it give to areas that are second or third? What message is given to the organization if the IT department are not the key drivers of such a high profile development? The message that is given out if out-of-house consultants are brought in should also be considered carefully.

Most people are not seeking influence as much as recognition and the opportunity to see their name in lights. They will see an Intranet as a means of either enabling this or depriving them of it. At best they will commit and drive the process, at worse they will actively fight against its progress.

The great debate within almost every organization is who has ultimate control of the Intranet development. A whole book could be written about the various techniques and methods used by power groups to gain control. The most common approach to overcome conflict is to elect champions from each department across the organization. The champion is not usually a dedicated resource but more of an ambassador who can represent the needs and priorities of their particular department. More is discussed about the role of content developers in a later section.

Unless managed within a framework (e.g. an Intranet Development Team or Steering Committee – see later), departments can see the Intranet as a battleground on which to enact their internal grievances and disputes with other departments. Communication can be destructive if it is allowed to be negative and in some instances we have seen Intranets as internal war zones where ongoing disputes are fought openly.

This is obviously an extreme situation, but it is rare for an Intranet not to tempt each department to act competitively. It is this energy that can be channelled to drive and develop the Intranet to produce bottom-line benefits. If each department is eager to be visible, it necessarily implies that they also need to be accountable. If a department's reputation is based on their responsibility for keeping their information live and dynamic, there is a naturally in-built system for the Intranet to work. This resource provides you with an existing means by which to achieve Intranet success.

It is naive to think that every department is going to have the same level of enthusiasm, time and resources to commit to making their Intranet section relevant and newsworthy. It is essential to understand who are likely to be the drivers and who are likely to put up barriers to the implementation. Early dialogue with appropriate representatives throughout your organization will offer a good feedback mechanism to avoid this problem.

Fear about loss of recognition and influence at all levels

within the organization

Beyond the departmental level within the organization, individuals will be keen to know how they and their colleagues work is represented. Is their work profiled or discussed? It is seen as strategic or tactical? Many will see the Intranet as a representation of the organization and any perceived neglect of their area of work as suggesting their lack of impact on the organization.

Often, sales information with particular reference to individual sales people is the first area which appears on an Intranet. We have seen this cause many individuals to feel extremely hostile. Typically it is individuals who resent the profile given to sales people or others who have missed the limelight for one reason or another.

Some organizations might argue that these feelings are positive as they either motivate individuals to perform better or lead them to direct confrontation with their immediate manager which then initiates useful dialogue and debate. Organizations that wish to avoid these issues will generally implement a policy that prohibits individuals being promoted or mentioned within the Intranet except to explain roles and responsibilities. Your organization should assess for itself the likely impact of this issue and introduce measures accordingly.

Fear of loss of employment across all levels of the

organization

This is indivisible from the fear of loss of recognition and influence. Anxiety over loss of employment is a key issue for any development like an Intranet.

Peter Drucker writes about the demise of middle managers when they become 'merely relays for the faint, unfocused signals that pass for communication'. If Intranets are to enable faster, clearer communication to filter through an organization, it isn't surprising that middle managers feel threatened. There is more and more evidence to suggest that improved communication through technology is cutting out the need for middle managers. Technology makes it easier to handle downsizing. Some examples of this are:

- If the technology is as easy as it appears, then what about the power bases for IT personnel built up over the last century. If software is easier to develop, will the IT remit lie in hardware and support, often seen as the least glamorous area of the industry.
- Remote working can significantly reduce the amount of sales support needed. In this instance, account management support personnel are likely to feel that their role is less significant to the organization.
- The classic personal assistant role has moved from secretarial support to an emphasis on proactive organizational support. Technology has reduced the need for secretarial skills as every modern manager is now expected to perform a significant percentage of his or her own administration.

It would be naive not to perceive an Intranet as a mechanism to tighten up the organization. Therefore in this context it must plan and handle the impact of reduced job certainty in specific areas of the business.

Assessing the business case

So how critical is an Internet to your business?

This can be expressed as to 'how critical is communication to your organization'. Intranets are merely a high tech solution for centralizing information and communication. The main issue surrounding Intranet developments is understanding what they are and what they can do.

The Value Chain Analysis (Figure 5.3) again proves useful here because it enables us to see where the communication interface takes place. With remote working and the increasing complexity of the sales process, the need for a strong communication channel between primary and secondary activities becomes crucial.

Organizations can use Intranets to increase the speed of communication across primary and secondary activities. In effect this liberates the organization to react faster, more efficiently and become more in tune with the marketplace.

It not only streamlines the interface across different functions but also increases the transaction speed of cascade to multiple layers in any organizational hierarchy. This can significantly reduce the negative impacts of strongly hierarchical organizations and improve consistency of information across flat management structures.

Next we outline the specific benefits in further detail.

Live communication so that everyone is 'singing from the same hymn sheet'

The delay in product development can cost an organization dearly in lost revenue. The delay in communicating product developments cost an even larger amount. Speed to market is a key variable in the long-term success of any organization. Therefore communicating quickly across an organization is becoming increasingly critical to competitive advantage and even survival.

Intranets are the ideal mechanism to communicate interactively with personnel responsible for sending the message out to the general public and specific customers. Traditionally large corporate communication budgets have been allocated to the task and the primary route to the consumer has been through printed material (be it on paper or CD). Pressure has been increasing for corporate communication departments to deliver results quickly and effectively. This has been particularly true of IT companies where speed of communication is as important as product development itself.

The major benefit Intranets bring is the two-way mechanism of communication. It is extremely hard to produce something in print

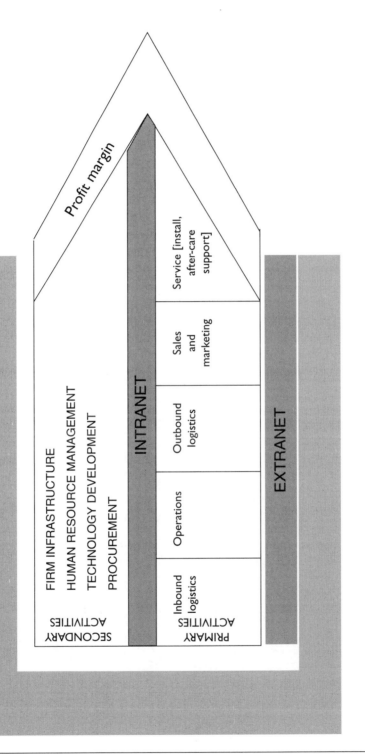

Figure 5.3 Intranet interface between primary and secondary activities

which actively addresses all the questions the recipients are likely to have. Internet technology enables both the publication of the message together with a channel to deal with any adverse reaction. This is most pertinent to strategic or cultural changes in the organization where emotions are involved but can also be applied to a new pricing policy which might conflict with existing discounts given to individual customers. Senior executives have peace of mind in that the speed of reaction is quicker in the worse case scenario and damage limitation can be exacted faster and with less impact in the marketplace.

The downside of this instant and interactive characteristic is that all feedback must be seen to be dealt with effectively. It demands that corporate communication departments become communication agents rather than publishers in the communication channel. Gone are the days when organizations sent down missives from the ivory tower of senior management.

Figure 5.4 Why ivory towers failed

The alternative takes longer, costs more, and is more frustrating but Intranets make it easier than before.

This also requires the same level of quality to be available so that personnel see it as important. Whatever negative aspects we can find in print as a medium, printed material requires investment and this needs to be signed off as correct and therefore carries more weight.

Information published in electronic format is cheaper and, because it typically has less rigorous quality standards, it necessarily carries less weight. Potential ways around this might include investment in the quality and the inclusion of video or live statements from senior managers. Signatures are another way of stressing sign-off and senior management commitment.

Global and intra-organizational communication

Beyond speed, coverage is central to understanding how Intranets can support your organization. Bar loud speakers, there has never been a mechanism that could transmit a message universally across the organization. With an Intranet, your organization has the ability to press one button and transmit one message uniformly to all employees.

The speed of the uptake of email installations from large to small organizations supports the fact that it delivers business benefits and delivers them fast. But the real benefits are gained when the communication is centralized, and a database of the communication developed. Companies can often find themselves repeatedly revisiting the same issues. New people want to make their mark and resurrect ideas which have already been rejected for sound business reasons. Centralized communication increases organizational learning and prevents the duplication of resources. Across a company with varying geographic boundaries centralized communication can significantly increase the adaptability, level of innovation and ability of the organization to provide profitable solutions and meet increasing customer demands.

Because the communication is centralized and visible to all it can act as a panacea to sensitive political issues. We say this very reservedly. What we mean is that often negative politics arise when people feel they are not given a voice. Intranets can provide a soap box or sounding platform for this and thereby enable positive action to take place in an open manner.

We are reserved about this because the politics take place on the creation of the system when it is decided who will be given a voice and how this is to be edited or controlled. In addition, it may appear as if there is the same amount of politics going on but it is even more visible on a computer screen. Much will depend on the amount of control programmed into the Intranet and how reactive measures are put in place to handle and confront any issues that are raised through it.

An example of a positive use of Intranets to reduce politics is the Delphi model of decision making. This model in essence involves how an issue is raised and then sent to all key recipients. Their response is added to the discussion in a publicly viewable manner so that all recipients can see everyone's opinion. The purpose is not to solve the issue but to brainstorm all the related issues, enabling everyone to access a broader context for the debate. The actual decision is usually taken by way of a meeting where those present have also taken part in the online debate. It has proved itself extremely effective in reducing meeting times and producing higher quality decision making. It also enables equal weight to be given to individuals with poor oratory skills.

On paper this sounds powerful, but the ability of technological tools must not be exaggerated to affect human patterns of work and emotional frameworks. The Intranet may not be able to address the conflicts and politics involved in any organization, but they can provide a common mechanism to address them. Specifically Intranets can standardize the language used across an organization. Having this common ground in language can enable a very large organization to feel smaller, cutting across cultural boundaries.

Cost of communication

Despite frustrations over ownership and control, organizations need to see cost savings as one of the most exciting opportunities of Intranets.

The reduction in the cost of communication is the major opportunity. Organizations spending significantly on dynamic internal communication can regard this as a primary motivation to adopt Internet technology. Printers, publishers and repro-houses are already beginning to feel the impact of this aspect of the technology.

Gaining feedback

Most organizations commission employee surveys when they already know there is an issue and are seeking to clarify its extent. This reactive stance stems from the fact that there is often a void between management and workers. Often, by the time an issue is identified it has already damaged the company to a certain extent.

Intranets can enable an organization to proactively collect employee attitude data to identify an issue as it is arising and before it impacts performance. This can be done formally or informally. Formally it might involve regular questionnaires (usually anonymous) which are consolidated and summarized for presentation. The key benefit here is financial because the technology reduces the costs of distribution and consolidation. The difficulty lies in what questions do you ask if you are trying to identify issues that may just be surfacing. Indeed by asking the question, you may actually risk prompting the issue to arise.

Informal data collection could be achieved through the use of open feedback forms, discussion groups and asking for contributions to an internal newsletter. Some organizations provide documents offering advice and asking for feedback about specific issues such as 'personality conflicts with superiors', 'departmental conflict' or 'quality issues being ignored by colleagues'. In this way a number of proactive steps can be taken to counteract negative impacts and forewarn decision-makers of imminent problems. This type of informal feedback mechanism, which prompts employees to give suggestions, can directly affect the bottom-line and improve business processes.

Collecting content

Most organizations launch their Internet site to find that three months into its promotion they are forced to provide further content. For large organizations, this can become a millstone around the marketing department's necks. Intranets provide a superb solution as they decentralize the responsibility of update. Many organizations have created Intranets for this sole purpose and committed personnel involved with front-line communication to contribute to the Internet site on a regular basis. This not only solves the problem of content creation but also leads to a greater sense of involvement and excitement about the Internet site. We discuss content developers in the next section.

The level of decentralization of content production is an important decision. At one extreme, any individual within your organization could then post content to a centralized area where some editorial sign-off process is in place. At the other extreme, the Intranet would be carefully managed by a core team of content developers representing specific areas of your business. They would then have full control over the content.

Knowledge capture and management

One of the most powerful uses of Intranets is in knowledge capture and management. This sounds grandiose but we simply mean the ability to capture what has been learned by the organization either from individual endeavours or as a team or organization. This could be as simple as learning why a direct mail shot failed to deliver the response that was expected, or senior management documenting why strategic decisions have been taken.

Every IT professional takes pride in documenting their programming. Indeed it is considered irresponsible for them not to because other people will also be working on the code. Not to document is to withhold the power base and make it harder for others to develop it further. Bug-fixes are also documented. Problems are expected with such a complicated piece of construction as software. These bugs are publicly demonstrated so that others can work around the defects. A simplified view of knowledge management is to go through this process for other business procedures, e.g. consultancy, quality, decision making. The onus is often on what has worked rather than what has failed because people's expertise is questioned when mistakes are openly documented but the concept remains the same.

The power of knowledge management within an organization is that it can explore issues more fully and adapt not to repeat previous mistakes. For senior management, there is a centralized collection point for paid knowledge acquisition over which it has intellectual property rights. For individuals revealing their knowledge bases, a rewarding representation of their efforts and achievements is generated. The downside is that historically people have retained knowledge bases in order to increase their own personal capital within an organization. They have used it to create a specialism for which they are respected and promoted. Sharing this knowledge can be viewed by protective individuals as reducing their net worth.

These issues have been skimmed over here and it is not the purpose of the book to go into great detail on how to use Intranets for effective Knowledge Management. Suffice to say that this is where the future of Intranets will lie over the next 10 years. We are already seeing Intranets being used for FAQs (Frequency Asked Questions) within organizations specifically aimed at induction training. They are also being used to capture technical support knowledge so that an improved customer support function can be provided by less qualified personnel. The key benefit is that it can be used to reduce information bottlenecks within an organization and improve customer service.

Employee motivation and involvement

Organizations who are prepared to open the floodgates of two-way dynamic information can be highly rewarded with improved employee motivation. People will be interested in issues where they can contribute. The more involved they are, the more motivated they will become to make informed decisions.

Remote working

Organizations who are prepared to develop an Intranet to the full extreme will easily see the business case for remote working. If all the internal systems needed for personnel to do their job can be accessed through an Intranet, the cost savings can be immense. These include travel expenses to and from the office, office space, office furniture and equipment, storage, support staff and a number of other overheads. The individuals themselves often produce better results and with good controls in place this can be visible within a short period of time.

Often the costs of developing supportive systems are high and there are usually a number of organizational barriers to confront such as fear of loss of control, reduction in social interaction, and anxiety about increasing isolation. Figure 5.5 presents an example

	Characteristics of the Intranet	Benefit	Costs
Presentation stage	Live communication	20 per cent reduction in newsletter print and distribution 30 per cent increase in speed of price change 20 per cent less photocopying	Increased disk storage needs Training staff on electronic publishing
	Global and intracommunication	30 per cent cost saving in international phone calls 50 per cent cost saving on international postage 5 per cent saving on international travel	Telecommunications investment high
	Cost of communication	5 per cent less on postage 20 per cent reduction in paper 30 per cent reduction in time distributing internal news/memorandums	
Interaction stage	Gaining feedback	Obtain earlier indications of opinion on organizational issues Product development timescales reduced by 10 per cent	Processing of feedback, 10 per cent of corporate communication personnel time
	Collecting content	Intranet to be self-maintaining by end of period	Content developers spend 30 per cent of their time building the core system; with 6 content developers, approximate budget is X
	Employee motivation and involvement	Suggestions box openly shown and management opinion can then be openly disclosed. 10 per cent reduction in staff meeting time	
Representation stage	Remote working	15 per cent increased productivity from sales personnel from reduced travelling time 10 per cent reduction in sales support time and personnel	Portable computers, software, support and telecommunications, approximate budget is X

Figure 5.5 Example cost-benefit analysis over a three-year time frame

cost-benefit analysis. Please note that any numbers given in this figure are used only for example purposes and depend solely on the nature of the organization being described.

Implementation

With Internet projects as outlined in Chapter 3, planning is everything and implementation is relatively simple. With Intranets, the opposite is true. Implementation is everything and planning should be limited to budget issues, goal setting and getting the right people involved to drive the project.

Intranets by their very nature are evolving systems that are continually being redeveloped in tune with the business. Starting by defining in detail all of the content and structure and then sticking to it (as you tend to with an Internet) is likely to constrain the business. As a business evolves and adapts its processes to the environment the flexibility of the Intranet system can become a key factor in an organization's ability to obtain and then maintain competitive advantage. It is common for the creativity of those who build and use an Intranet to evolve business processes and enhancements that directly impact upon the organization. The personnel involved must understand the potential for direct benefits to their department and the business and be sufficiently motivated to bring the system into common usage.

A large IT development structured to include an initial specification stage followed by a period of construction and then finalized by a single stage of installation, while necessary for certain projects, has some inherent flaws. It is this approach that can result in IT systems created to solve yesterday's business problems. The adoption of rapid prototyping where a demonstration of the finished system is presented back to those non-technical staff who will eventually use the system, has reduced the number of misunderstandings contained within the initial specification. This approach can improve the chances of delivering a system that encompasses all those expecting to be involved. However, the fact that the development takes place out of the immediate environment where the system will be used means that there is still often a gap between the system's functionality and the business needs. This gap is often visible in the frustration between business professionals and IT staff. However, by making an Intranet development take place in the work environment it is possible for business professionals to enter the sacred world of IT and at last bring immediate efficiencies to bear on their departments and jobs.

Successful Intranets become a seamless part of the infrastructure of an organization. The procedures used and modified become a normal part of daily business life and provide the ideal illustration of how the most successful Intranet systems are created and used. As with written procedures business professionals and the users of the Intranet should be able to enhance and modify the Intranet within the work place.

Build a little, use it, build a little more ...

In order to create an environment that will trigger this type of evolutionary development the initial Intranet project should be scaled down. The target is to build a little then use it within the organization and build a little more only once convinced of the need for it. By scaling the project down into separate Intranet projects, it then becomes practical to undertake the development within the business environment. At various points all those who have to use the Intranet can then make suggestions for improvement.

Often at the start of Intranet projects, business professionals perceive it to be the solution to all their business and communication issues. This 'over-romanticized' view of Intranets means that their expectations are greater than what is likely to be achieved in the short term. This naiveté needs to be pre-empted and managed by strategic people in the organization. In the worst case it can lead to guerrilla warfare tactics by departments who seek to control the mechanisms to do their job and undermine the underlying IT infrastructure which is crucial to core business activities. Managed at a strategic level within an organization, this desire can be effectively channelled into an open and constructive debate between business users and IT professionals and a system can be created which adds value to the core IT infrastructure and to the business.

The other danger area is if this over-romanticized view of the technology is allowed to impact negatively on the change process, which occurs during the implementation of an Intranet. There is usually a natural hostility towards upheaval in most organizations because people like to feel a sense of job security and too much change can easily threaten this. As a result, there is usually an immediate decrease in effectiveness and efficiency as this change process takes place. If this is right for the organization, the decrease in business benefits is soon counteracted and the overall impact is profitable and constructive. It is up to key strategic management to ensure that the cost of the change process is kept to a minimum and the benefits of the change process occur quickly. If the technology is not over-romanticized and managers are aware of both the positive and negative impact, the benefits of Intranets can be obtained faster and more effectively.

It is also crucial that management commitment is gained from the outset and that they are aware of the potential damage caused by the change process. It often has to get worse before it gets better. It has been known in many instances for key management not to have been involved enough during the planning process. When the negative impacts of change then occur, it is these key managers who are most likely to reject the process and revert the organization to its original way of functioning. If there is real management commitment, with a solid belief that it will work, then it will (assuming that the change process is right for the organization).

Motivational issues on implementation of Intranets must also be managed throughout the organization. Figure 5.6 shows a typical profile of expectations plotted against time during a change process.

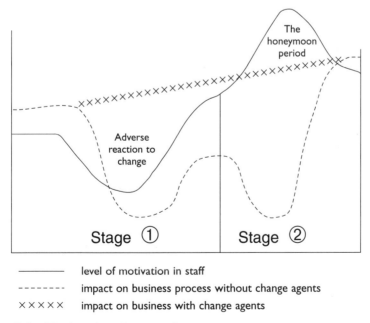

————————	level of motivation in staff
- - - - - - - -	impact on business process without change agents
× × × × ×	impact on business with change agents

Figure 5.6 The benefits of using a change agent

- **Stage 1.** At the start, personnel do not expect the Intranet to radically change the way that they do their jobs. As the opposite proves true, there is a sharp decrease in motivation and commitment to the business. We title this 'adverse reaction to change' in Figure 5.6. This will be exacerbated if not planned for and pre-empted.
- **Stage 2.** If key personnel are involved during the process, they will soon begin to deploy the technology appropriately and the status quo will return. The balance then tips to the other extreme and it is common for key personnel to want to go further and become interested in the potential of deploying the technology further. The impact of both the negative and the over-positive are equally disruptive to business processes. Therefore the business experiences two disruptions – one from adversity to change and one from what we have entitled 'the honeymoon period'.
- **Stage 3.** Either personnel are involved in deploying the technology further or their interest is moderated in other ways. The business process gets back in-line at a more efficient and more effective level than from the outset.

Use of change agents

The most effective way to deal with these issues is to involve external change agents. They have tools and techniques for managing and minimizing the negative effects of change.

Their major contributions are to minimize the harmful effects of opposition to change and harness the positive aspects of the honeymoon stage whilst limiting its damage to the business.

The fact that these individuals are outside your business means that personnel have a safe, unbiased route to channel their anxieties or enthusiasms for the change process. The change agent's role is effectively to smooth the process and ensure that negative issues are pre-empted and well planned for. Empowering the agents to take control of the process means that the internal politics do not further complicate or exaggerate the effects of change.

Intranet implementation consultancy is 90 per cent change management and 10 per cent business process re-engineering. We stress this because if the 90 per cent of change management is effective, key personnel who are at the root of the business will seamlessly adapt the technology to match the needs of the business.

Risk assessment, technology and creating an information management system

So knowing the typical profile and impact of the Intranet, the decision now is how much risk is your organization prepared to take? How far should the Intranet be used to modify the business and how it functions? This is where the Cyberstrategy Model comes into play and the next section looks at the potential benefits and risks associated with each type of development of Intranet technology.

At this point we are faced with the technology. What should we use to bring the Intranet into existence and how should it be managed? We recommend that the organization invests in the set up of an Information Management System and a large part of this chapter is dedicated to explaining what this is and why it is important.

Intranet representation

We start with Intranet Representation because it holds the greatest benefits and risks for any organization. There are many terms used to describe this stage, such as:

- the paperless office
- the virtual organization
- remote working.

Effectively it is the total reverse of the classic head office model, which is a centralized system where individuals seek to control information and communication. The head office is effectively replaced with the Intranet.

- Opportunities. Representation is where the organization's business processes take place within the Intranet and can be accessed remotely. Some organizations move directly to this stage. They aggressively deploy the technology to represent essential business processes. The key rollout is usually in the following order:
  - Marketing: remote access to product information and marketing literature
  - Sales: remote access to customer information
  - Accounting: remote access to financial information.
- If the technology is deployed aggressively, departments playing coordinating or communicating roles can be cut immediately. Individuals relaying information can be replaced by the technology. Office space can be

drastically reduced. The cost base is therefore totally re-engineered giving your organization the ability to increase profits or compete on reduced prices whilst retaining margins.

- Radical deployment of Intranets has resulted in organizations achieving significant competitive advantage. Intranets provide the opportunity for organizations to be smarter, leaner and more adaptive to the needs of the marketplace:
  - Number of employees can be significantly reduced.
  - Cost bases reduce substantially and so do the costs of maintaining the cost space, e.g. building maintenance, cleaners, office machinery, etc.
  - Operational staff are not constrained to the physical location of the office.
  - Communication is faster, easier and cheaper. People spend less time communicating and more time producing results.
  - Business processes are speeded up because the reporting and information channels can be reduced.
  - Organizations can be flatter without reduced management control.
  - Empowering individuals is made easier and less risky because Intranets can make business processes more visible.
  - Empowered individuals with easy access to information means that meeting customer needs is easier and customer service will increase (assuming the people are right).
- Risks. With rapid deployment of Intranets at the core of the organization, change effects are significantly higher risk. The diagram given earlier (Figure 5.6) has more pronounced curves; the negative aspects of the change process has the potential to stop the business functioning. The honeymoon stage is more pronounced when individuals have the opportunity to develop their own systems and procedures and bypass the core.
  - The business depends solely on the technology, it is the means be which the business trades. If the technology fails to deliver so will front-line staff and so will the business. It is dependent on good IT people.
  - The effect on staff can be immense because they will be made redundant or transferred elsewhere in the organization. They will be made more visible and more accountable.
  - Customers may suffer during the change process and may go elsewhere.
  - The organization is dependent completely on good strategic management and effective change agents.
  - The comfort factor of seeing and touching tangible evidence of busi-

ness processes is reduced: office capital is less; teams of people in one office may well disappear; the use of paper will be significantly less.

Intranet interaction

A centralized information system, which creates a meaningful dialogue with employees, is a good starting point for companies that are more risk averse. It enables an organization to plan the move to Representation and flesh out the problems of doing so in advance. It also smoothes the people aspects of the change process.

- **Opportunities.** Interaction is where the organization centralizes the communication process and encourages active dialogue between departments and individuals. It separates a flatter communication structure and therefore faster business processes to occur.

  If the technology is deployed aggressively and uniformly, again departments playing coordinating or communicating roles can be cut immediately. This type of implementation has seen the end of information managers, account support roles and marketing communication managers.

  However, only the communicational and information aspects of the business are optimized through this route. The Intranet fails to support every business process and therefore there is an opportunity to have a huge impact on the cost structure of the organization.

  – Communication is faster, easier and cheaper. People will spend less

Nullifire

www.nullifire.com

Nullifire, an intumescent paint manufacturer, had a 20-strong telesales and account support function. It implemented an Intranet which centralized all project and customer information with remote access. Orders could be placed and invoices raised remotely. Within two months of the project, remote sales people needed significantly less communication with the core Nullifire telesales team. Sales levels increased and not only was the investment in the Intranet recouped but 10 of the account team could be deployed more effectively. Office space, which was at a premium, was freed up and after an initial decrease in morale, the organization became smarter, leaner with a higher committed work force.

time communicating and more time producing results.
- Management information is obtained more easily.
- The information gap between managers and personnel is reduced.
- **Risks.** The risks are significantly less. People will perceive improved communication as a positive outcome so the diagram shown previously (Figure 5.6) will have less pronounced curves. The honeymoon stage may have a more pronounced effect as personnel see the impact of the technology and recognize the potential of representation. Unless the expectations of this stage are handled well, key bright knowledge workers may well feel short changed and strategic managers may feel that the disruption would have been better rewarded by more radical steps to actually change the way the business operates. The change agents in this case will be more focused at managing the expectations of the honeymoon stage.

The only real risks of this stage are:
- Employees highlight the negative aspects of the business and management must be seen to control and react to this.
- Employees use the communication mechanisms to communicate more at the cost of producing less effective results. With the organization producing a visible communication tool, the cultural values of the organization may inadvertently change to rewarding people who communicate rather than perform.
- Good management communication will become evident and visible but this will also highlight inadequacies in management to communicate effectively.

Intranet presentation

This involves the least risk but carries none of the core opportunities of those highlighted previously. It does not impact the business in any of the ways highlighted previously. In effect, the Intranet becomes an organization wide notice board. It is a useful facility to save the costs of cascading information through the organization but the implementation will not develop the business.

- **Opportunities.**
    - Cascade corporate information quickly and uniformly around the organization.
    - Centralized and easily accessed information especially for remote workers (e.g. quality, procedural and training manuals).
- **Risks.** None except internal time resources.

Multi-stage or big bang?

Is it better to evolve through Presentation to Interaction then to Representation, or move straight to the latter stage? It is extremely difficult to generalize because which route will be best is highly dependent on the organizational culture and existing structure. We can, however, provide some issues which can help in this decision process.

	Opportunities	Risks
Presentation	• Cascade corporate information quickly and uniformly • Centralized and easily accessed information	None except internal time resources
Interaction	• Communication is faster, easier and cheaper • Management information is obtained more easily • The information gap between managers and personnel is reduced	• Negative feedback from employees • A 'talk rather than do' culture • Highlights the quality of management communication
Representation	• Reduced number of employees • Cost bases substantially reduced • Operation staff not constrained to the physical location of the office • Communication is faster, easier and cheaper • Business processes are speeded up because the reporting and information channels can be reduced • Organizations can be flatter without reduced management control • Individual can be empowered • Business processes are more visible • Levels of customer service increase	• High dependence on technology • Huge impact on culture and employee morale • Effect on customer relations • High dependence on good strategic management and effective change angents • Reduced comfort factors – reduced tangibles

Figure 5.7 Summary of opportunities versus risk

- Representation involves a significant amount of IT migration and re-engineering. This can be conducted in parallel to the development of an interactive Intranet. This would support an evolutionary process.
- If speed to market is an issue then one change process may well be better than two or three stages.
- If the organization has high levels of IT and staff are computer literate it may be advisable to let the organization plan the implementation of their own migration independently by setting the overall date and objectives of the transition. This is particularly relevant when departments use outside IT contractors to develop their applications.
- Service companies are the most likely to be able to move rapidly to a Big Bang approach. They may find that their industry is already forcing them down this route and they do not have the luxury of an evolved staged process.
- Manufacturing companies are typically poor implementers of back-office technology and therefore may find themselves in a position of being able to make a quantum leap straight to Representation specifically because they are starting from a greenfield situation.

These are the kinds of issue that will influence which is the optimal route for your organization to pursue.

Technology considerations

The first question that needs to be addressed is whether you intend using the Internet as the mechanism by which remote workers access the Intranet. The main advantage to this route is that it is extremely cost effective. Remote workers will only be paying the price of a local telephone call to access the Intranet no matter where they are in the world (assuming that they are using an international access provider). The set-up costs for the organization are also much less than creating a private network. The disadvantage is that the Internet is a public network and therefore complete security cannot be guaranteed. There will be a risk even with good encryption technology and this must be weighed up against the alternative costs.

We would recommend that any organization faced with this question should consult specialist consultants who will be able to cost the alternative costs of either private network or Internet and assess the security risks.

Smaller organizations are unlikely to be able to afford the luxury of their own private international network. However, if they are not expecting large (greater than 20) numbers of simultaneous users, a private network simply means in this case a centralized server which a modem can access rather than using the Internet. The costs for this method will be higher because each user will be charged national call rates outside the local area.

The next decision is whether to outsource the management of the technology. Complete ownership and control would seem to be the obvious route with something as critical to an organization as its Intranet. However, there is a strong business case for having the technology managed remotely both from a cost and effectiveness perspective.

Third-party suppliers and management of Intranet technology have the following benefits:

- They have expert skills and will agree service levels which you depend on.
- There are advantages in shared telecommunications infrastructure, with significant economies of scale by a supplier investing in significant telecommunications rather than your own organization trying to develop its own.
- It enables you to focus on core business and does not impinge significantly on your IT resources.
- They will be able to offer you 24/7 (i.e. 24 hours a day, 7 days a week) support.
- You will have increased security because the machine isn't in your building.
- Your server is set to automatically send information to this server at regular intervals.

A remote machine managed by a third party may be robust and well controlled but it must also have seamless interaction with a machine within your organization. Effectively it becomes a gateway to your organization and therefore good supplier tendering and negotiation is essential. We recommend that this is done at both strategic and technical levels of the organization.

Just like any outsourcing issues, this decision will be highly dependent on your current level of skills and resources. It also greatly depends on your preference for control and ownership. What is known is that more and more large organizations are pursuing this route and it is proving to be more effective and better value for money. However, as soon as personnel need to access systems which are not Internet compliant, then your decision is automatically reversed. You would then be better advised to develop an internal server within your building and to invest in your own telecommunications.

The decision tree in Figure 5.8 highlights some of the key issues.

The most important issue concerning this technology is that it must provide a robust solution, which must also facilitate a managed process for modifying and enhancing the system. This will greatly depend on which stage of development the Intranet is at.

Technology implications for the development of a presentation Intranet application

Because Presentation is only interested in publishing information, the only technical requirement is that users each have a browser on their machine and all have access to a centralized server. If there are no remote workers, there may not even be the need to have a dedicated Intranet server. You could simply keep all the information on the centralized server and point every user's browser in the organization at the home page of the Intranet. The information contained within the Intranet can simply be produced using a word processor, which will save documents in HTML (Internet) format.

One step up from this would be to have the home page professionally designed and word processor templates created so that there was a standard look and feel to the Intranet. This is an efficient way of producing a high quality look to the Intranet without recourse to the costly involvement of outside agents.

Technology implications for the development of a interaction Intranet application

Because Interaction is about inviting response, it would be extremely difficult not to employ a dedicated Intranet server. Here the software needs to be progressed beyond browser displayed pages and move into server-based functionality such as response forms and databases. This needs to be linked closely with email so that information can flow smoothly around the organization.

It is not in the scope of this book to review all the Intranet or GroupWare (as it is sometimes called) software. What we must cover is the concept of replication or subscription which has become

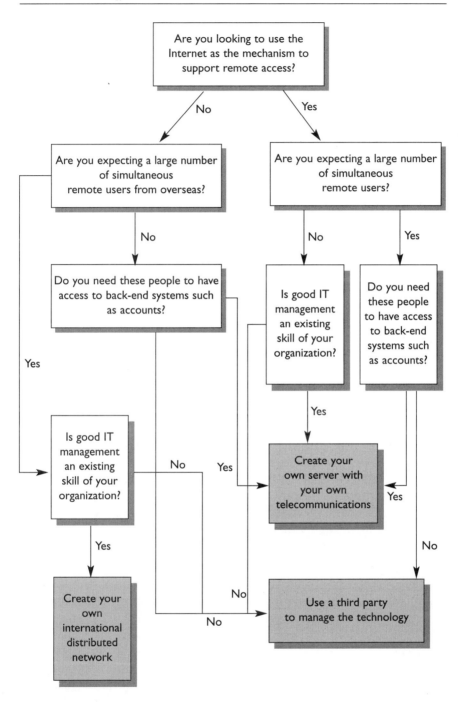

Figure 5.8 Decision tree for implementation of internal technical infrastructure

a key characteristic of this technology and a major ingredient in creating an Interactive Intranet.

The major problem associated with users accessing information from a centralized machine is that they have to have access through a modem dial-up if they are outside the organization. A common business requirement is for users to be able to collect information and use it remotely when not connected. The problem with this is that they will want to amend information, but then also have some way of updating the centralized copy. The first most popular solution to this problem came with the origination of Lotus Notes in the early 1990s. This system enables replication and has the ability for locally stored information to be compared with centrally held information and the latest copies of each swapped so that both locations then contain up-to-date versions of all documents.

This replication technology is at the core of any Intranet, which purports to be Interaction because it enables remote users to keep and work on remote copies of the information. It enables them to interact and keep the information dynamic whilst also making a contribution to the application while disconnected from the central system.

Technology implications for the development of a representation Intranet application

An organization migrating all of its IT infrastructure into a Representation Intranet is highly dependent on the key suppliers providing the existing systems. Most large software houses are addressing the issue of how to make their software Internet compliant but obviously the development will not take place overnight. Most organizations compromise with data import and export facilities, which are made automatic. This is the easiest short-term solution.

The central issue for this type of implementation is the level of organizational housekeeping. It is common for Intranets to become disorganized even after a short period of time unless there are sufficient management and controlling mechanisms put in place at an early stage.

We now discuss a key recommendation of the book and describe an information management system. Although we have chosen to highlight this specifically here, it may also be relevant to Intranet Interaction if the implementation is large.

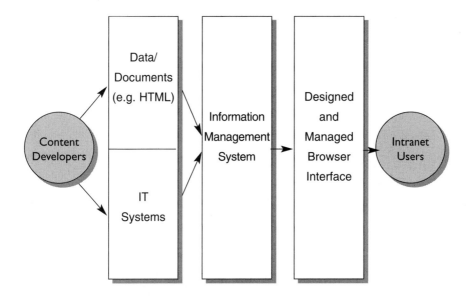

Figure 5.9 The relative position of an information management system

Creating an information management system

In effect, an information management system (IMS; Figure 5.9) is the interface between the core data and technology and the end client. It acts as the process by which the data is transformed into information, which is then manageable and easily controlled.

The processes and systems are not simply administrative but are also essential to produce an Intranet which is robust, reliable and correctly updated with pertinent and timely information.
It consists of:

1 Organization structure – roles and responsibilities.
2 Quality procedures and systems – keeping the information current and accurate
3 Security – protecting the information.
4 Legal – laying down the rules and constraints.

Organization structure – roles and responsibilities

We recommend setting up an **Intranet Steering Committee**. This committee would encompass all key personnel responsible for content development within the Intranet. (In addition there will be the Intranet Project Manager together with a Webmaster; both are described below.)

The purpose of this committee is to:

- share and learn from each others' experiences
- collaborate on projects
- propose, plan and coordinate new developments
- manage the overall structure, navigation and objectives of the overall site.

The committee should meet on a regular basis, e.g. monthly, and describe both the work completed to date as well as future developments. The role of the Intranet Project Manager is to chair these meetings and ensure that all participants are encouraged to contribute and share experiences. The key is to create a development environment in which learning is accumulated rather than reinvented and lessons are learnt across organizational boundaries.

Developing the role of the **Intranet Project Manager** will be an extremely important contribution to the long-term success of the Intranet enabling its eventual rollout into an Extranet.

The overall purpose of the Intranet Project Manager is to manage the development of the Intranet such that it continues to add value both to your personnel and potentially to a wider external target audience.

As projects are proposed at the Intranet Steering Committee, the Intranet Project Manager would coordinate the development. Major tasks are to:

- ascertain the budget implication and ensure there are sufficient funds to cover the project – this may either be from within the department or from a centrally held budget
- ascertain whether it conflicts with any other activity which is planned on the IT side or within the business generally
- ascertain the scope of the project and the organizational impact
- define the exact scope and objectives of the project
- agree a project plan for implementation and monitor the development

- obtain authorization for the project
- police the development in terms of adhering to the procedures and systems set up
- arrange or coordinate the necessary level of user training, education or communication.

We would recommend that another responsibility of this person is the management of the Webmaster.

The **Webmaster** can either be an internal or external resource. This role is to provide technical infrastructure and support to your Intranet project. This role may be supplied externally by a third party if considered appropriate.

As projects are proposed at the Intranet Steering Committee, the Webmaster would advise the team upon the technical implications and options. He or she would then implement the necessary technical systems. The main tasks are to:

- write server programs or scripts to perform the necessary tasks on the Intranet
- maintain and upgrade the server
- email administration
- provide technical support for all users of the Intranet
- assess, propose and implement the adoption of new technology
- educate the Intranet Steering Committee on the implications and opportunities of new technology
- communicate and work in partnership with designers and the creative team behind the Intranet design.

In some cases the Webmaster may have sufficiently advanced skills to undertake the design and creative features of the site. In most cases, it is preferable to use a separate design support service. This can be from an in-house design team or outsourced.

Many organizations choose to use an external agency to produce the Intranet design and image, which can then be maintained and policed by the Webmaster. Briefed well, it is our experience that early Intranet design which is approved by all members of the Intranet Steering Committee can be rigorous in the long term and extremely cost effective. The key saving is that the design retains impact without recourse to designing every new page that is added to the Intranet. We discussed the design implications of the Intranet in Chapter 2.

Content developers are personnel tasked with the role of creating content for their department/division of the organization. They will need sufficient knowledge of the technology but need not have advanced technical skills. Their contribution will be through the creation of content and functionality for the Intranet that will effectively communicate knowledge and information across the organization.

These people need to act as champions for the Intranet within their particular department or division. They take complete responsibility for the content provided and for the accuracy and timeliness of the information.

Although the overall direction they wish to pursue is directed and agreed at the Intranet Steering Committee, the day-to-day maintenance of the information is managed decentrally by the content developers. This would entail:

- internally agreeing what information should be published on the Intranet which then leads to the practical implementation of:
  - adding pages
  - modifying pages
  - deleting and archiving existing information which has outlived its shelf-life
- suggesting new developments or changes to the navigation system and structure to the Intranet Steering Committee
- obtaining departmental budgetary approval for developments or putting forward proposals for centralized funds to be allocated
- liaison with the Webmaster for technical support for all developments
- liaison with the Intranet Project Manager in respect to project management and changes to the agreed development plan.

Quality systems and procedures

In order to facilitate a seamless working of content developers within a centrally controlled Intranet site, certain quality systems and procedures need to be in place.

When adding new pages, every new page added must be referenced with:

1 Who created the page?
2 On what date?
3 A 27-word description of the page for displaying within the Intranet search facility and for ease of reference and access.

4 The date on which the page should be deleted. A program/script can then be written by the Webmaster for automatic deletion.
5 The status of the page. This includes Waiting for approval, Internal use only, Can be viewed by suppliers, Can be viewed by clients. This will become more and more relevant if the Intranet moves towards becoming an Extranet but in the short term can be used for editorial sign-off by relevant people. This status will be linked to the security such that pages are profiled against permitted access rights.
6 The reviewer's name. This could be the Intranet Project Manager or Department Head that signs off the content as appropriate. If acceptable, certain Content Developers may be given authorization to sign off their own content but we recommend that a procedure for sign-off is agreed and a facility for this in place at an early stage so the movement to Extranet is easily accomplished.
7 The reviewer's sign-off date. This is the date that the page was reviewed and signed off by the reviewer. It may be necessary also to include a comments area to enable the reviewer to feedback comments about the page but at this early stage a simple fast sign-off procedure is the minimum needed to ensure a quality check is in place.

When modifying existing pages the same information as above will be embedded in every page but in addition modification information will also need to be tracked as follows:

1 Who modified the page?
2 On what date?
3 What is the new version number of the page?
4 Why it was modified?
5 Who reviewed the modification and on what date?

When deleting pages there are two options. The pages can either be deleted from the Intranet completely or archived in an historical database. Your organization needs to decide whether there should be a standard in place where all information is archived when no longer relevant or whether the decision to delete or archive should be left to the discretion of the Content Developer.

On deletion or archive the following information must be stored:

1 Who deleted/archived the page?
2 On what date?
3 Why it was deleted/archived?

Security

Security is of course the most serious consideration on implementation of the Intranet. Although facilitated by the technology, the security considerations are for the information contained within the Intranet and this is why it forms a key aspect of the information management system.

Security is three fold:

1 Security against external interference or access to the Intranet. This is facilitated by a plethora of hardware and software (routers and firewalls) provided by a number of suppliers. It is inappropriate to enter into the security debate in this book. The central feature to remember is that the ultimate security goal is to avoid any external access either out or in. This is why in most instances Intranets are set up, managed and maintained internally. Remote working is facilitated by dial-up through a private telephone number.

   Beyond this you are using the Internet as a public network to transfer organizational data. There will always be a security risk. The decision needs to be made at a senior level whether the risk is worth the tremendous cost savings and benefits of using the Internet. If there are doubts raised, the safest option is not to use the system for highly confidential material but to rely on existing internal communication channels for these.

2 Securing the data and information against loss especially pertinent to off-site data. Another area where there is a potential security risk is the fact that with remote working, organizational data is often held remotely. Especially with replication technology, a modern portable is capable of holding the complete data-set for the whole organization. This combined with the chance of a portable being stolen must be planned for and security measures put in place to protect the data on any machine located remotely. We would recommend a comprehensive security policy is put in place and all personnel forced to adhere to strict procedures and systems.

3 Security – appropriate levels of viewing the information. This is often not considered important on launch of an Intranet as it is often perceived to be a company-wide, open system with no restriction on access. However, it is our experience that once the organization tries to move from Presentation to Interaction, there will be data which your company may not want viewed by all employees. At this stage there are significant costs associated with engineering security into an existing open system. Therefore, we recommend building this in from the outset.

Presenting different views of the Intranet in terms of security is critical for senior management buy-in as they can see the forward capability of a system that will enable suppliers and partners to access the system further down the line. The potential is there for the Intranet to be rolled out as an Extranet.

Different security levels can be used to offer tailored or personalized views of the Intranet. These can place different emphasis on specific sections depending on the profile of the user. In this way, senior managers offered management information on entry to the Intranet; sales personnel can be provided with sales targets and performance markers on start-up, etc.

Legal and policy

We recommend that the legal implications of internal electronic publishing are clearly identified, content developers briefed and information provided online inside the Intranet.

We cannot stress enough the importance of checking your legal position before going live. The Appendix gives some points and guidelines but, if you have any doubts, it is paramount that you seek legal advice.

We also recommend particular attention is focused on the issues of:

- **Copyright.** No third-party material (text or graphics) must be published on the Intranet without the express permission of the owners of the material.
- **Defamatory information.** No negative information pertaining to competitors or other organizations must be published unless it is publicly available information. Intranet published material carries as much weight legally as Internet published material.
- **Pornography.** There must be a clear statement that this will not be tolerated and disciplinary action will be taken by any persons publishing or circulating this material in any way.
- **Personal use.** A policy must be agreed as to whether your organization allows employees to use the Internet for personal use, whether this is constrained to out of work hours or whether it is not permitted in this context.
- **Links.** There is a hidden assumption of recommendation when your organization creates a link to another organization's Internet site. Even with disclaimers for liability, an employee may buy or take decisions based on this inferred recommendation. If the employee then falls into difficulty, your organization can then be considered responsible.

Therefore, centrally your organization must agree whether links to Internet sites are permitted. If so, it must the responsibility of the Intranet Project Manager to ensure that these links are endorsed by your organization.

Corporate identity and design

Many Intranets fail not on content but because of the user interface. Organizations recognize the importance of planning an easy to use and cosmetically appealing Internet site which clients will visit usually for a maximum of 15 minutes. However, many organizations decide not to invest substantially in a user interface to an Intranet which may be used eight hours a day by a significant proportion of their employees.

We consider the design and corporate image of the Intranet to be one of the most important considerations for the following reasons:

- The design can often become a political battleground and it is more cost effective to agree the design up front across the organization than to incur the expensive costs of redesign as each department wishes to make a bolder statement than the previous.
- A strong, flexible design will be an investment which should last for a significant time period.
- A design which involves framesets or templates makes adding information easier and more cost effective as the design is built in at the outset rather than relying on design within each page.
- Users will either find the Intranet easy and attractive to use or not. If they have had an initial bad experience on using the Intranet, it will be much harder to encourage and regain interest and enthusiasm.
- Implemented well, it can add significantly to the internal perspective of the brand and corporate image. Our experience shows that it adds a huge amount to the 'feel-good' factor of an organization and increased levels of corporate loyalty.

The role of the Intranet Project Manager is to gain consensus on the overall design and structure of the Intranet across the whole organization. We do not underestimate the political complexity of this activity but believe that this is the most important starting point for a professional implementation. Thereon, the Intranet Project Manager plays the important role of policing this corporate identity and pulling into line any department or division that deviates.

It can be useful to employ outside agencies at this initial stage of developing identity and design for the Intranet because they bring fresh innovative ideas and can often neutralize the effects of internal politics. If they have developed a number of Intranets for other blue chip organizations they will be adept at identifying ways of representing the front end (home page) to the satisfaction of all parties. They can also plan how the navigation system will enable easy and fast access to pertinent information.

The key to getting the design right is to ensure that it reflects the corporate image and message of the organization and that there is significant user involvement in the decision-making process. We recommend that the Intranet Steering Committee is responsible for briefing and creating the Intranet design.

This structure of an Intranet can be identical for all three types of Intranet development. The key difference is in the interactivity of the information (Interaction) and whether is integrates with the core IT applications within the business (Representation).

- **Internal systems** – quality manuals, procedural manuals, personnel procedures, resource booking or availability
- **Internal communication** – email, telephone directory, corporate communication, internal newsletter, surveys and questionnaires
- **Client relations** – client list/database
- **Product/services** – product information and flyers, manuals and specifications, price lists, new products
- **R&D** – new development and requests for research
- **Sales and marketing** – sales material, brochures, newsletters, client newsletters, competitive information, market trends
- **IT** – manuals, developments, tips, technical support, frequently asked questions
- **Finance** – performance figures, accounts, purchase/procurement, order book
- **HR** – internal contact directory, role and responsibility overview, internal policies, e.g. holiday, sickness, etc.
- **Fun** – organizational events, charity raising initiative, where to go in the surrounding area, gossip database
- **News** – stop press items of immediate interest.

Training and education

The role of the Intranet Project manager is to ensure that both the content developers and the internal target audience using the Intranet have sufficient technical skills in order to make the application successful.

We recommend that in addition to internal technical training, you instigate an educational process that highlights the benefits and objectives of the Intranet. Without this Intranets can often be seen as an additional work item which fails to add value to each employee's job roles and responsibilities.

We would recommend that all employees attend a one-hour launch seminar about the Intranet. The seminar should explain how the Intranet will be used, highlight all aspects of the content, future plans and explain a process whereby individuals can request developments to the Intranet Steering Committee.

Maintenance

With Internet developments we recommend the ratio of three times the amount of development spend to be budgeted for maintenance of the system per year. With Intranets, the development of them should be integrated seamlessly into the business so that they should not represent an obvious or significant pull on resources.

However, the initial inertia and enthusiasm input at the launch will drain remarkably when it comes to keeping the information updated. Here the glory has gone and mundane routine takes over. This is especially true for information systems involving resources like competitor or market information, which unless made interactive can be time-consuming to keep dynamic.

If data does fall into decay the key question must be why. It is usually one of the following reasons: either the inputter(s) are not obtaining any direct personal benefits or the organization is not. In the latter case, the solution is simple, delete the database and keep a hard copy which people can access if needed. In the former, management must decide how critical the information is and find some tangible way of integrating the input into the jobs of those involved and reward them for their contribution.

Maintenance must also be seen as a strategic issue and senior managers must be seen to be using the system as a communication channel. The quickest mechanism for killing an Intranet is to lose senior management involvement. Therefore it is important that the senior managers are consulted by the content developers and are seen to be encouraging the process and enabling sufficient resources to be allocated to the project on an ongoing basis.

Outside consultants for maintenance

Another key decision in respect to maintenance is whether to involve outside consultants. The benefits can be found in two areas: adding content and design to the Intranet and the most appropriate deployment of the technology.

- Outside agents for content. Professionally produced content for the Intranet demonstrates commitment to the system as a core communication and educational process within the company. This is particularly useful when outside agencies are already used to create the content for traditional communication channels.
  - PR companies who produce press releases can be contracted in to provide updates to the news section of the Intranet.
  - Leasing companies can be contracted in to provide car policy guidelines within the Intranet.
  - Training organizations who make products designed for Intranets.
  - Outsourced knowledge acquisition from information providers. There are information providers who will provide Intranet feeds directly into your Intranet. The benefit to your organization is that a third party is providing dynamic information, which is increasing the level of knowledge within the company. The relative costs can be surprisingly small when compared to the costs of allowing each individual to source material or expertise elsewhere.
- Outside agents for the most appropriate use of technology. No matter how technically proficient your existing IT resources and skills are within the organization, there is always a vast range of technologies which could potentially add value to the Intranet. Potential suppliers will have deployed the technology in a more innovative and appropriate way and can offer ideas that could continue to drive the initial inertia into even further bottom-line business benefits.
- The rapid growth of Internet technology means that you would need a dedicated resource allocated to spotting technology which might address specific organizational needs that arise. Even with this resource, you may still lack the practical know-how to apply new technology in the most appropriate way. These issues summarize why ongoing Intranet consultants are central to the long-term success of the project.
- You should choose a supplier who is constantly implementing leading edge and successful Intranet implementations. The contract you would

make with this supplier would be to provide quarterly reviews with the Intranet Steering Committee where recommendations for development would be written as a report after consultation with the group.

What next?

Once the structure, content and management system of an Intranet is created and integrated into the everyday working of your organization, you are now ready to roll out the system either to a select audience (Extranet) or to the general public (Internet) (see Figure 5.10).

The advantages of going to A, B or C is that the development is controlled and prototyped before going to the general public within D, E or F. It is important that we do not underestimate the power of Extranets as they are likely to encompass the core business activities of the organization as it stands today. The only real advantage of going to F rather than C is that it enables you to tap into customers you do not already know.

The greatest business benefits are to be obtained from going from 3 to F. This could involve taking an internal ordering system out to suppliers and then out to the end customer. In this way, a retail system could be linked directly to suppliers and the organization is confident that the processes work because the processes have been built outwardly from core operational systems.

It is almost impossible to give case studies in this area as all,

	Internet	Extranet	Intranet
Presentation	D	A	1
Interaction	E	B	2
Representation	F	C	3

Figure 5.10 Options for developing on from an intranet

without exception, reveal business processes that organizations would not want in the public domain. Needless to say, retail and distribution organizations are seeing movement in the direction of 3 to C and then to F as critical for their long-term commercial viability. It is no longer a question of 'if my competitors will follow this route' but 'when are my competitors going to take this route'.

Conclusion

Intranets are merely a tool to increase company-wide systems and communication for improved business processes. They can be extremely powerful when implemented and supported at senior level. However, there is still a huge amount of technical marketing hype surrounding the industry. This can often detract from the sound business case behind developments that will generate a planned Intranet strategy that incorporates the correct systems and procedures to sustain long-term improved business processes.

On the Internet

Live on the Internet at www.marketingnet.com/cyberstrategy/intranets we offer you:

- links to organizations we have highlighted and case studies examined in this chapter
- links to other high quality information about this subject available on the Internet
- the ability to discuss your experience of Intranets with the authors and other readers of *Cyberstrategy*
- the ability to post a question to the *Cyberstrategy* community

References

Drucker, P. F. (1994) *Innovation and Entrepreneurship*. Butterworth-Heinemann.

Nussbaum, K. (1987) Office Automation: Jekyll or Hyde? *Social Insecurity: The Economic Marginalization of Older Workers*. 9 to 5 National Association of Working.

Chapter 6

Conclusion

Competitive advantage comes from an organization increasing efficiencies or effectiveness in the value chain over and above competitors. This book has provided you with all the tools and models for you to diagnose how networked and Internet technology can assist your organization in this process.

One of the most interesting aspects of the advent of this technology is the depth and spread of both its opportunities and its threats. For some industries it holds the key to competitive advantage alongside the key to decline. Even in the most traditional products, the Internet is lowering international boundaries and enabling new entrants to come in more easily.

They can support, add value and reduce costs across the whole value chain. They can enable you to gain competitive advantage or obliterate your position in the supply chain. Within the organization, they can improve morale and productivity. They can enhance all aspects of communication and most of all they can help you re-engineer the way that you conduct business today.

This book has provided you with ideas and conceptual models to think about how your organization fares in the hostile competitive forces model shown in Figure 6.1. But the picture is constantly changing and as organizations smarten up the way they work and communicate both internally and externally, they are using this technology to re-engineer their organizations – to reinvent themselves. Your industry will constantly be changing in this regard.

Cyberstrategy has provided you with tools, ideas and a framework to take any of your concerns from concept into implementation. We would appreciate your feedback about how successful the model has been for you, simply email the authors at strategy@marketingnet.com. Alternatively, if you feel comfortable sharing your opinions with other readers, we invite you to take part in our on-line forum at www.marketingnet.com/cyberstrategy

Lastly, may we wish you the greatest success with your Cyberstrategy in both the short and the long term.

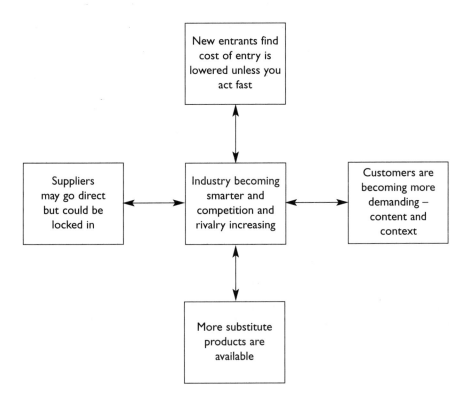

Figure 6.1 Competitive forces acerbated with Internet technology

A guide to legal issues

This Appendix has been written by Rachael Bickerton, a lawyer in the Computer, Communications and Media Group at Lovell White Durrant (London, UK).

Foreword

The comments in this Appendix are intended to increase awareness of some of the issues of law and the Internet. This is not an exhaustive list and should be viewed merely as a guide to some of the issues surrounding the Internet. The law is developing in this area as quickly as the technology itself. This is no substitute for specific legal advice.

Advertising

There is no legislation in England which specifically addresses advertising on the Internet, although there are specific rules concerning certain products, such as financial services or pharmaceuticals. There are also self-regulatory codes and rules, such as those of the Advertising Standards Authority (ASA).

The British Code of Advertising Practice and the Sales Promotion Code, published by the ASA's Committee of Advertising Practice, set out a number of principles that must be complied with by all advertisers. The rules apply to advertisements on computer and video games, CD-ROM and the Internet as well as press, poster and cinema advertising. The general requirement is that advertisements must be legal, decent, honest and truthful. Furthermore, advertisements must not exploit the 'credulity, lack of knowledge or inexperience of consumers' and should not mislead consumers through inaccuracy and ambiguity, exaggeration, omission or otherwise.

The ASA supervises these codes on a system of self-regulation. Although the codes do not have the force of law, failure to comply will result in adverse publicity (as ASA rulings are published monthly). The ASA can also refer a persistent or deliberate offender to the Office of Fair Trading (OFT) for legal action under the control of Misleading Advertisements Regulations 1988. The OFT may seek an injunction in court to prevent such misleading claims in advertisements.

The ASA publishes a booklet, *Interactive ASA*, which is a useful reference tool. The ASA also publishes its adjudication and codes on the Internet and is useful because it enables companies to obtain pre-publication advice as to whether an advertisement will comply with the ASA codes. The ASA site can be found at www.asa.org.uk

Specific rules may apply to the advertisement of certain products. For example, the use of the Internet as the advertising medium for financial services does not alter the fact that the relevant legislative provisions must be complied with.

There is also legislation to consider, such as in the UK, the Trades Descriptions Act 1968, the Consumer Act 1974, the Prices Act 1974, the Unsolicited Goods and Services Act 1971, the Consumer Protection Act 1987 and the Trade Marks Act 1994. Also, other relevant regulatory bodies and their codes may have to be considered. For example, the Financial Services Authority has stated that a lot of financial services advertising comes within their regulatory regime, and there are several voluntary codes on advertising and/or interactive marketing issued by the International Chamber of Commerce and the Direct Marketing Association.

Distance selling

The sale of goods and services concluded over the Internet (distance selling) is subject to specific rules in the ASA codes. The European

Union Directive on the Protection of Consumers in respect of distance contracts will also apply. The Directive was published in 1997 and is to be brought into force in the UK and all other EU Member States by June 2000. Amongst other things, the Directive requires that the customer must be provided with certain information, has a seven-day withdrawal period (without giving any reasons and free of charge) and his or her order must be satisfied within 30 days. Some types of distance contract maybe exempt from the application of the Directive, such as financial services. (There is however, also a proposal for a Distance Selling Directive in the context of financial services.)

Jurisdiction

The issue of who can be sued, and where, is highly problematic and complex. For example, what if an employee of a French company posts a defamatory comment concerning an English company on an electronic bulletin board for which the service provider is a German company but its URL is .com? Should the action be brought against the employee or the company, and in which country should the action be brought? Each case must be considered on its own facts and, in many instances, the answer will depend on the laws of that country. As a general rule, the best jurisdiction in which to sue is that of the infringer, where they may have some assets to enforce your judgment against. However, bringing proceedings in a foreign court can be fraught with difficulties. It would be worth consulting a local lawyer to check out the position.

The issue of which laws apply to a web site must also be considered. It is obviously impracticable to seek advice and ensure compliance of a web site in every jurisdiction although, in theory, the contents could be downloaded in any country which has Internet access. This means that material would then be subject to local consumer protection, defamation and trade mark laws (to give just three examples of problem areas). However, you should consider where your major target audiences are located and then consider issues such as advertising and contents compliance in terms of those countries. Of course, the country where your server or the server of your Internet service provider must also be considered.

A site that is not considered obscene in one country may be in another and therefore might be potentially actionable. You may wish to include disclaimers stating that the site is subject to UK law and only open to UK residents.

Defamatory, obscene, discriminatory or harassing material

Both material on web sites and contents of email may be actionable for defamation, racial or sexual discrimination, obscenity or harassment due to their contents. Steps should be taken to monitor and vet web sites and bulletin boards and a written corporate policy should be implemented to make it clear to visitors and to staff that they are not allowed to post or circulate materials of a defamatory, obscene or harassing nature.

If it is intended to set up a web site that enables third parties to post material that can be read or viewed by other people, for example by providing electronic bulletin board or 'live chat', steps must be taken, both through monitoring and by including a warning on the site, to ensure that offensive actionable materials are not posted.

Even internal e-mails run the risk of causing significant financial loss to a company, if sued upon, particularly if the email then gets into the hands of an external third party. In July 1997, Norwich Union apologized and agreed to pay Western Provident Assurance £450 000 in damages and legal costs for defamatory statements, originally distributed on its internal email system, which spread rumours that the private health group was in financial trouble. The danger of internal email is accentuated by the fact that people tend to treat email as a relaxed and informal means of communication.

It is also important not to include on a site or in an email any materials that might be regarded as sexual or racial harassment. In practice, this is more likely to arise in an Intranet than in relation to a web site. Various cases in America have been well publicized. One law suit filed by two African-American Morgan Stanley employees concerned an internal email containing racist jokes. The case was settled, but the settlement sum is likely to have been large as the employees initial damages claim was for $30 million each. Another US harassment action was brought by a woman over a joke ('Why beer is better than women') that circulated the internal e-mail system, which she found offensive.

It may also be prudent to set up a corporate policy to search the Internet for information about your own company in order to locate, and take swift action in relation to, any defamatory or otherwise damaging comments on other web sites.

Intellectual property rights

When preparing a web site, a number of legal issues relating to intellectual property rights (most particularly copyright and trade marks) must be addressed.

Copyright ownership

Once material is placed on the Internet, the owner of intellectual property rights in that web site effectively 'loses control' in that site in so far as it can be downloaded, copied and redistributed without consent. Consideration should be given to not putting certain copyright works on the Internet unless you are prepared to lose control of it. All sites should contain a copyright notice and an explicit licence setting out the extent to which the material may be copied or circulated, although this obviously does not prevent actual copying. In addition, the appropriate copyright symbol with the name of the entity that owns the copyright should appear on the web site, with the year in which the copyright came into being. It may also be preferable to include a copyright symbol in some sort of footer which appears on every page. Users should be prohibited from altering or modifying material on the web site unless its owner wishes them to do so. Under English law, it is a criminal offence under the Computer Misuse Act 1990 to cause an unauthorized modification of the contents of any computer, which is likely to include modification of a web page.

There may also be technological ways to protect your copyright including some form of embedded message in the text, rather like a watermark, that would require great effort to avoid or delete it. It may be worth 'finger printing' a site, to see who has visited it, and also to encrypt works to ensure that a downloaded version may only be used if the downloader has a key to decrypt it. Similarly in respect of software programs, it may be worth inserting an innocuous but erroneous line of code, which can be traced in copies of the program.

Use of a third party's copyright

If the web site owner proposes to put materials or software created by third parties on the Internet, even if it has used that material before this does mean that the web site owner is entitled to use the same material in other circumstances. Generally, a licence is granted to use copyright works for a specific and limited purpose. For example, a licence to use a photograph in a magazine or in a press advertising campaign may not extend to its inclusion in an electronic publication, even if of the same magazine. The fact that a company has used a piece of music in a television or radio campaign does not mean that it is entitled to use the same music or photograph in conjunction with a web site. Any use of third party material must be cleared in the normal way and, where it has already been licensed for use, the extent of that permitted use should be checked to ensure that the intended use is covered.

It should also be remembered that many different rights may apply to the material in question and, as such, the consent of several rights holders may be required. In the case of soundtrack, for example, the composer may own the right to the music, the producer of the record may own the right to the recording and the performers may own the right to the actual performance.

Software licences

When using existing software licences to exploit a web site or in conjunction with a web site, the web site owner must consider whether or not the existing licences permit this new use or whether they are fairly specific as to a particular machine, web site or purpose. Similarly if the software is bespoke, companies often think they own it because they commissioned and paid for it, but the company must ensure that it does own the rights in that software. If there is no agreement to the contrary, title and copyright belongs to the author, unless written by an employee in the course of his or her duties. Even if a company has commissioned a copyright work and paid for it, but has not obtained a written assignment of the copyright ownership, it will either have been granted some written licence in the development documentation or it merely has licence to use the software and it is unlikely to be able to transfer an implied licence to a third party.

Hypertext links

Care should be taken when providing a hypertext link on a web site. In the UK, the issue of whether providing a hypertext link is copyright infringement has not been decided. In the *Scottish Shetland Times* case, the judge found that copying headlines from a newspaper's web site to create hypertext links into that site was arguably a copyright infringement. The case settled before a full hearing was heard. The *Shetland Times* generated revenue for its web site newspaper from advertising on its home page seen by users when visiting the site. The plaintiffs were particularly concerned because the hypertext links provided by the defendant's site, *The Shetland News*, enabled visitors to access those stories directly without passing through the *Shetland Times* home page, thus bypassing their advertising.

When providing a hypertext link, you may consider acknowledging the site owner to which you are linking. Part of the settlement entitled *Shetland News* to link the stories, providing that they had an acknowledgement underneath each headline stating that it was 'a *Shetland Times* story' together with the *Shetland Times* masthead logo.

One must also be careful in selecting a hypertext link, if that site may be liable to contain material which could be defamatory, obscene, etc., or in breach of a particular regulation. It would be worth making clear, on the web site, that when leaving that site by a hypertext link, the controller of that site takes no responsibility for anything done as a result of visiting the second site. Some regulatory bodies have even gone as far as to recommend this – more than one regulator in the financial services sector has done so. If a company proposing setting up a web site operates in a regulated environment, it is worth checking what the regulator may have said on use of the Internet as a delivery channel.

Trade marks/passing off

If using a web site to promote a company's 'brand' or 'image', it would be worthwhile to register any trade marks or logos at the Trade Marks Registry. It would also be useful to continue to monitor the use of the branding, particularly if a lot of time and money has been invested in the 'corporate image'. Deviations from the way trade marks and logos are presented and alterations to the marks themselves could dilute their distinctiveness and affect their validity, particularly as electronic commerce expands.

There may be countries in which a company has not registered its trade marks. As a consequence, it may be possible, although hopefully remote, that someone locally may have registered a mark which could lead to a local trade mark infringement. It is important, therefore, to establish the countries of your target audience and to consider obtaining registrations in those countries.

Care must be taken if using a competitor's name or logo. Comparative advertising, usually to promote one product at the expense of another, may, amongst other things, amount to trade mark infringement if it is not used in accordance with honest practices in industrial or commercial matters and the advertiser takes unfair advantage of or is detrimental to the distinctive character or repute of the competitor's trade mark. Furthermore if there is a misrepresentation to a prospective customer, calculated to injure the business of another trader and which actually causes damage, the competitor may have an action in 'passing off'.

Domain names

It is possible, for an owner of a trade mark to prevent a third party using that mark as a domain name. For example, Harrods obtained an injunction requiring various defendants to transfer to Harrods all rights they held in the domain name Harrods.com. Hopefully the recent

One-in-a-Million case in 1998 has put an end to the practice of 'cybersquatting' (domain name grabbing). One-in-a-Million registered domain names such as marksandspencer.co.uk and spicegirls.com with US, UK and other domain name registries and tried to sell them to potential users. The High Court held that this was both passing off and trade mark infringement.

Disclaimers

Web sites should carry a health warning in relation to accuracy, reliability and fairness. Furthermore if it is intended that access to material on the web site should be restricted, password protection may be necessary.

Other disclaimers may also be advisable. As with terms and conditions, a balance must be struck on how that health warning/disclaimer is presented. A link to a disclaimer or terms and conditions hidden at the bottom of a home page in small print is less likely to be enforceable than those which a user must scroll through each time it visits a site and click on an 'accept' button before entering the site.

Data protection

If any dealings with individuals via the Internet or email systems involve holding and processing data on computer relating to individuals on computers, data protection registration must be obtained. Both the purposes to which the data will be used, to whom it will be disclosed and, if applicable, the intention to transfer the data outside the UK, must be registered. If a user is not registered, it commits a criminal offence. The Data Protection Bill is due to be enacted by October 1998 to give effect to the EU Data Protection Directive and to replace the current Data Protection Act 1984. The basic rule, under both the current legislation and the Bill, is that the information held about living people must be obtained and processed fairly and lawfully. When obtaining such information, customers and potential customers must be told the identity of the data user (i.e. the company who will be holding and processing that data, the purposes for which the data will be held or used and those to whom the data may be disclosed). Therefore where data, such as a customer's name and address is to be provided over the Internet, the web page must make the relevant information clear. Indeed, under the new Bill consent to processing personal data may be required in certain circumstances. The Bill introduces quite a few changes on the use of data about living individuals and web site owners should familiarize themselves with these.

In addition to the requirement to warn data subjects where a system is not secure, certain principles of good practice in relation to personal data apply. The Bill provides that (subject to certain exceptions) the data subject's explicit consent must be obtained, when processing 'sensitive' personal data such as data on racial or ethnic origin, political opinions, religious or philosophical beliefs, trade union membership or health or sex life.

If such information is contained on a database, the database or parts of it may attract both copyright and database right protection. A person infringes a database right if, without the consent of the owner of the right, he or she extracts or re-utilizes all or a substantial part of the contents of the database. The database right is a relatively new one (it came into force in December 1997) and companies with valuable databases should familiarize themselves with the new law.

Where personal data is being sent via the Internet by 'ordinary' email, the user must be warned that the Internet is an insecure medium and that the user's privacy cannot be guaranteed. If some sort of security is offered for the data, the level of encryption available for such information, for example, could determine whether or not a warning notice is appropriate.

Forming a contract

The issue of when a contract is formed over the Internet has raised much debate. Under English law there are four essential elements to a contract: offer, acceptance of the offer, intention to create legal relations and consideration (the purchase price). An advertisement on the Internet is generally treated as an 'invitation to treat' (if worded correctly) rather than an offer, so that the advertiser may be entitled to turn down an application from a potential customer. The application by the potential customer would be treated as the offer which the web site owner does not have to accept.

If selling products from a web site, it is important that the terms and conditions underpinning the transaction are referred to and available for the customer to read. These may well be distinct from the terms and conditions governing access to the site. Ideally, as with disclaimers and health warnings, the potential customer should be obliged to scroll through the terms and conditions and immediately prior to the finalizing a transaction confirm that he or she has read them and accepted them. They should, at the very least, be referred to prominently on the first web page with a hypertext link to the actual terms and conditions. When designing a web page it is important to ensure that the customer cannot circumvent the 'accept' dialogue box by, for example, book-marking the final page and going straight to it at a later date and avoiding the 'accept'. This is particularly important if the terms and conditions change in the interim.

The law is currently not settled as to when acceptance of the offer occurs and thus the contract is formed – is it when the offeror sends an email confirming the customer's order or when the customer receives that communication? As the law is unclear, it is advisable it should be made clear in the relevant terms and conditions or by a statement that will be seen by the customer before sending an email, that the contract will not be formed until the web site owner has received the email accepting its offer.

Certain types of contract may only be formed once they have been signed. At present, it is likely that the English courts will not recognize a digital signature in those instances where a signature is required by statute or even by rules of self-regulatory organizations (e.g. Investment Management Regulating Organization, IMRO) require that customer agreements must be signed.

Business communications

It is also worth noting that, under the Companies Act 1985, the name of the company must clearly be stated on all its letters, notices and other official publications, bills of exchange, promissory notes, endorsements, cheques and orders for money or goods, invoices, receipts and letters of credit. A company failing to comply with this is liable to a fine. The Business Names Act also requires certain information to be contained in business communications. A web site owner may also need to comply with the relevant professional codes and rules. For example, the Solicitors' Investment Business Rules requires that a firm involved in the conduct of investment business is to state on its business communications that it is regulated or authorized by the Law Society to do so. Therefore, a template should be prepared, to be used every time an email is sent to a recipient outside the company, automatically adding the information required by law and perhaps a confidentiality warning as well in relation to disclosure of the contents of the email.

Confidence

The general law of confidence will apply to both data held on a computer system and manual data. It will apply to confidential data sent over the Internet to a web site which is then used without the authority of the provider of the information. It may well have been sent for a specific purpose but the web site owner may use that data for a purpose beyond the authorized use. The general law of confidence applies to corporate confidential information as well as data about living persons.

Three elements must be established for an actionable breach of confidence to exist; information must be of a confidential nature, which has been parted in circumstances creating an obligation of confidence and there must have been an unauthorized use of that information to the detriment of the confider (although later case law suggests that this may not be necessary at least between private litigants). Breach of the duty of confidence may entitle the aggrieved party to obtain an injunction to prevent further misuse and / or claim damages.

The increasing danger of the use of the Internet is that, once confidential information is in the public domain, it is no longer actionable. The ease with which information may be disseminated throughout the world by, for example, the creation of hypertext links, means that if an action is to be taken for breach of confidence, it must be taken quickly, before the confidential nature is lost.

In using information relating to individuals, consideration must also be given to the individual's rights to privacy. Although there is no general law of privacy in the United Kingdom, there are certain specific pieces of legislation that address the privacy area and the European Convention of Human Rights, which provides a right to privacy, is currently being incorporated into our domestic law through the Human Rights Bill.

Implications of discovery obligations

If a writ is issued against some one, that person/company comes under an obligation not to destroy documents which might possibly be relevant to the action. If the company has in place a system for the deletion of email files after the expiry of a fixed period of time, it may find itself inadvertently in breach of this obligation. Procedures should be put in place to avoid the possibility of such an occurrence. The obligation to preserve documents and to disclose them arises in any litigation. Staff should, accordingly, be required to act with caution when sending emails, not simply to minimize the company's exposure to a claim for libel or other action over the contents of the email, but also to avoid prejudicing the company's position generally with regard to litigation in which it is involved.

Index